Copyright @

Andy Clark

Published by Works Publishing

While every precaution has been taken in the preparation of this book, the publisher assumes no responsibility for errors or omissions, or for damages resulting from the use of the information contained herein.

THE ART OF MEDIEVAL WARFARE: STRATEGIES, TACTICS, AND WEAPONS OF THE BATTLEFIELD

First edition. February 20, 2024.

Copyright © 2024 Andy Clarke.

ISBN: 979-8224796533

Written by Andy Clarke.

Table of Contents

The Art of Medieval Warfare: Strategies, Tactics, and Weapons of the Battlefield..................1

Introduction..................3

Part 1 | Chapter 1 Objectives and Campaigns 6

Chapter 2: Armies and Their Composition 17

Chapter 3: Strategic Deception and Intelligence 26

Part II: Medieval Battle Tactics | Chapter 4: Cavalry: The Shock and Awe 37

Chapter 5: The Infantry: From Shield Walls to Pike Blocks 51

Chapter 6: Siege Warfare: Breaking the Walls 64

Part III: Weaponry and Technology | Chapter 7: Blades and Polearms: Close Combat 73

Chapter 8: The Bow, Crossbow, and Beyond 85

To my wife and kids , i thank you.

The Art of Medieval Warfare: Strategies, Tactics, and Weapons of the Battlefie

Introduction

Clashing steel, the thunder of hooves, the desperate cries of the wounded – the image of medieval battle is embedded in our cultural consciousness. Popular depictions often emphasize its chaotic and barbaric nature, painting a picture of warfare dominated by frenzied violence and brute strength. While these elements were undeniable aspects of life and death on the medieval battlefield, the reality of war in this era was far more complex and nuanced. It involved a tapestry of strategy, tactical innovations, technological advancements, social changes, and above all, human ambition interwoven with the raw struggle for survival.

Medieval European warfare was far from static. Its landscapes were dynamic stages where a dance of destruction and cunning took place. This was an age of profound transition. It was a time when knights, whose martial dominance was once unchallenged, found themselves vulnerable to disciplined archers and massed infantry. Feudal levies, often poorly trained and equipped, gradually made way for more organized and professional armies. Stone fortresses, once bastions of absolute power, found their walls shattered by siege engines of increasing sophistication.

However, beneath the veneer of popular misconceptions about medieval warfare lie surprising and compelling examples of tactical brilliance. Commanders and armies across Europe adapted to a changing landscape of military power and emerging technologies. They demonstrated surprising levels of sophistication on and off the battlefield. It's crucial to remember that the clash of arms was fueled by much more than a thirst for conquest. Political maneuverings, religious fervor, the defense of homelands, or simple greed – motivations ran deep. Therefore, warfare itself demanded thoughtful and well-laid plans. Success didn't hinge on brute force alone, but also on careful analysis and calculation.

This book transcends the myth of mere barbarism and exposes the multifaceted nature of medieval combat. We venture beyond castles, knights, and swords to uncover the strategic minds that manipulated them. We will look at the broader military landscape of the era, examining logistics, the composition of armies, and the way societies mobilized for war, painting a complete picture that goes beyond simple combat. It was on these battlefields that strategies bloomed and tactics evolved, laying a foundation for military practices even in the modern age.

But make no mistake, this won't be a sterile, bloodless exploration of medieval conflict. We will delve into the heart of battles, chronicling the development of devastating weaponry, from the bone-breaking mace to the armor-piercing longbow. We will explore the rise and fall of fortifications, understanding how stone giants rose to defend kingdoms and met their end brought by siegecraft born from ingenuity and destructive power. The raw courage and brutality of combat alongside the tactical genius of the age intertwine to form a compelling and bloody tableau.

Moreover, warfare cannot be separated from the realities of its time. From mounted charges to infantry clashes, and siege warfare's slow burn, these were the stages shaped by the rigid social hierarchies and technological limitations of the period. Therefore, understanding medieval warfare demands we recognize how both battlefield prowess and tactical failures emerged from this distinctive tapestry of society and war.

It isn't simply about reconstructing what was. This book seeks to reveal the 'why' of medieval combat, uncovering the motivations that fueled war, and the consequences that lingered long after the dust settled upon

THE ART OF MEDIEVAL WARFARE: STRATEGIES, TACTICS, AND WEAPONS OF THE BATTLEFIELD

the battlefield. While popular media fixates on the flash of a sword or the thundering charge, we will dive deeper to expose the strategic calculations, the cunning deceptions, and the desperate gambits that truly sculpted victory and defeat on the medieval battlefield.

As we embark on this journey, prepare to leave behind the myth of medieval warfare as an uncontrolled exercise in brutality. Instead, a canvas painted with innovation, strategy, ambition, and human resolve emerges. We will witness an era where tactics and technology clashed alongside the unquenchable ambitions of kings, and where soldiers carved their names in history – or met their end – on fields shaped by cunning as much as steel.

Part 1

Chapter 1 Objectives and Campaigns

The Various Goals of War: Conquest, Defense, Raids, and Religion

The clash of arms on the medieval battlefield was rarely a random eruption of violence. The reasons for warfare in this era were multi-layered, with ambitions both lofty and base driving nations, factions, and individuals into conflict. Understanding the complex web of motivations is essential to grasp the intricacies of military decisions, strategies deployed, and their larger impact on societies.

Conquest: The Hunger for Land and Power

Perhaps the most obvious driving force behind warfare throughout history is the desire for conquest. From ambitious kings to aspiring petty lords, the lust for dominion fueled countless campaigns. Medieval Europe, a mosaic of evolving kingdoms, duchies, and fractured realms, was a fertile ground for conflicts born from an unending thirst for territory. Expansion offered resources vital for growth – fertile lands, control of trade routes, and an increased population providing both taxes and a base for military recruitment.

Conquest extended beyond just taking control of physical territory. Campaigns could be launched to gain dominance over a rival ruling house, subdue rebellious vassals, or lay claim to disputed titles. Victorious monarchs not only increased their domains but also reinforced their position within the hierarchies of power and prestige.

Defense: An Age of Perpetual Threat

While conquest is proactive, defense played an equally important role in shaping medieval warfare. In an era without strongly defined borders

THE ART OF MEDIEVAL WARFARE: STRATEGIES, TACTICS, AND WEAPONS OF THE BATTLEFIELD

and centralized nation-states, protecting existing territories was a continuous concern. Threats could come from external empires seeking new lands to rule, neighboring lords with an eye for expansion, or even a power grab by rivals within a divided kingdom. Fortifications like castles were built not simply for displays of dominance but as bastions against relentless threats.

The necessity of defense meant armies weren't simply offensive tools. They held the responsibility of maintaining territorial integrity and protecting the inhabitants who relied on them. Battles driven by defense could be desperate acts of preservation or well-planned tactical maneuvers designed to inflict losses unsustainable for invaders.

Raids: Profit, Revenge, and Disruption

Not every medieval conflict was about grand campaigns of conquest or desperate stands of defense. Localized wars took the form of raids – smaller-scale incursions that often blurred the line between criminality and state-sanctioned warfare. Such raids were fueled by greed, the desire for swift material gain, the need for supplies, or a calculated move to weaken and demoralize an adversary. Frontier regions within a kingdom or areas bordering rival states were particularly susceptible to these hit-and-run attacks.

While raids could be opportunistic events, they also factored into larger military strategies. Burning crops, harassing supply lines, and capturing livestock acted as precursors to broader invasions, undermining an enemy's capacity to resist. Such acts might even force rival armies to break off sieges or engage in hastily planned battles meant to halt the destruction the raids wreaked.

Religious Motivations: Faith as a Weapon

Medieval Europe was a world defined by faith. Crusades, those sweeping wars sanctioned by the papacy, offer the most visible example of religion intertwining with warfare. The defense of Christendom or the liberation of holy places became powerful ideological tools for fueling war. It promised earthly rewards alongside spiritual ones, motivating kings, commoners, and adventurers alike to take up arms, even in far-off lands. Religious fervor offered a common cause that extended beyond feudal obligations and local concerns.

But warfare driven by faith wasn't limited to large-scale Crusades. Conflicts could erupt across Europe sparked by religious discord between Catholics and various dissenting groups or conflicts based on struggles for power within the very structure of the Church itself. Religion could ignite civil wars, fuel rebellions, and drive nations into prolonged wars in the name of perceived piety and the upholding of faith.

Warfare's Unifying Threads

Despite these distinct motivations, certain underlying factors were omnipresent. Medieval warfare was often deeply enmeshed with concepts of personal and dynastic honor. Avenging insults, real or perceived, or settling a grudge through victory on the battlefield was a driving force behind even smaller-scale conflicts. Battles were viewed as proving grounds for valor and reputation, where a leader's worth was measured alongside the loyalty of their followers.

In the complex tapestry of medieval history, warfare was never a mere act of violence confined to the battlefield. It had profound economic underpinnings that intertwined with the political, social, and cultural fabric of societies. The costs of raising and maintaining armies were staggering, requiring vast resources and manpower. Armies needed to be equipped with weapons, armor, horses, and supplies, placing a significant burden on the economy. Additionally, the disruption caused by military campaigns had far-reaching consequences. The movement of armies ravaged the countryside, destroying crops, pillaging villages, and disrupting trade routes. This could lead to famine, disease, and economic decline in affected regions.

On the other hand, victory in warfare could bring significant economic rewards. The spoils of war included captured territories, treasure, and resources, which could greatly enrich the victorious party. These spoils could be used to fund further military campaigns, strengthen fortifications, or invest in economic development. However, defeat in warfare could have devastating economic consequences. The vanquished often faced crippling burdens of debt, as they were required to pay reparations to the victors. This could lead to a decline in living standards, social unrest, and political instability.

The long-term impact of warfare in the medieval world extended far beyond the immediate aftermath of battles. The outcomes of wars shaped and reshaped the intricate dynamics of power and territory. Victorious rulers expanded their domains, consolidating their power and influence. On the other hand, defeated rulers might lose their territories, titles, or even their lives. The redrawing of political boundaries and the shifting of power balances had profound implications for the lives of ordinary people.

The bloody machinery of conflict left an indelible mark on the lives of those directly involved. Soldiers risked their lives on the battlefield, facing the horrors of combat and the possibility of death or injury. Civilians were often caught in the crossfire, subjected to violence, displacement, and hardship. The psychological and emotional scars of war endured long after the fighting had ceased.

Campaign Planning, Logistics, and the Importance of Supply Lines

Beneath the surface of clashing armies and legendary battles lies a complex realm crucial to medieval warfare – that of campaign planning, logistics, and the often-undervalued importance of supply lines. It is in the mundane calculations of provisions, routes, and costs that the fate of entire campaigns, even kingdoms, could be secured or irrevocably lost.

Campaign Planning: Beyond Swords and Strategy

The image of a brilliant commander deciding troop movements on a battlefield map captures only a fragment of medieval campaign planning. Before armies ever marched, an intricate and delicate dance of preparations took place. This was a domain ruled by practicalities as much as strategy, where war councils involved factors far removed from the romantic notions of battle.

Choosing the right time of year was essential. Harsh winters or impassable terrain during rainy seasons could cripple campaigns before any enemy was encountered. Kings and advisors had to analyze intelligence reports on enemy dispositions, assessing the ideal time to strike – when an opposing force was perhaps divided, preoccupied elsewhere, or weakened due to poor harvests.

Campaign objectives were critical. Whether a long-term goal of conquest, a more focused raid, or the relief of a besieged city, objectives dictated the scale of preparation involved. Recruitment efforts had to match the expected manpower needed, along with the resources necessary to arm and supply them. This, in turn, determined the financial realities of waging war – loans might be raised from wealthy merchants, taxation could be increased, or religious institutions pressured to support the cause.

Medieval planners could rarely take the easy route. Strategic considerations had to account for a network of roads and waterways that were vastly different from today's standards. Rivers meant fording, and bridges became either valuable tactical objectives or potential

THE ART OF MEDIEVAL WARFARE: STRATEGIES, TACTICS, AND WEAPONS OF THE BATTLEFIELD

chokepoints. Mountain passes might create treacherous bottlenecks or offer the means to surprise a complacent enemy. The need to scout not only enemy dispositions but the suitability of potential battlefields and pathways adds yet another complex layer to this multifaceted tapestry of preparations.

Logistics: The Invisible Army

"An army marches on its stomach," goes the often-used adage, a reality medieval commanders understood acutely. Logistics – the art of moving, supplying, and sheltering troops – was not merely an optional aspect of warfare, but a force multiplier or a recipe for swift disintegration. Armies on the move consumed vast quantities of food, fodder, and resources. Planning campaigns without securing these necessities doomed armies to defeat before a single arrow flew.

Medieval logistics faced inherent limitations. Armies largely traveled on foot, with baggage, weaponry, and siege equipment transported by cumbersome ox-drawn carts. Foraging played a vital role, but could only sustain an army for limited periods, especially given the destruction a hungry multitude could visit upon its path. Therefore, military planners focused on securing supply depots along calculated routes. Securing these required their own logistics and defenses. Moreover, armies frequently lived off the land, commandeering local supplies with little regard for the needs of the population, fueling animosity and sparking rebellions throughout history.

Transport of war engines and construction materials for siege weaponry posed an additional and formidable logistical challenge. Planners could rarely depend upon local workshops. Thus, blacksmiths, carpenters, and skilled laborers traveled with armies, forming crucial logistical components in themselves. Their tools and materials increased the logistical burden yet could prove the linchpin for success.

The Tyranny of Supplies

Supply lines weren't simply lines on a map, but arteries upon which campaigns lived or died. They formed targets for daring raids or desperate gambits aimed at starving out a besieging army. Conversely, severing the logistical lifelines of an advancing army could prove more powerful than meeting them in an open battle. For defenders, disrupting the enemy's supply lines and foraging was a crucial element of warfare, sometimes proving far more decisive than the heroic defense of besieged towns and castles.

Weather had a cruel say in supply matters. Rivers, vital lines for transporting the heavy machinery of war, could become unnavigable due to drought or winter freeze. Storms at sea could sink supply fleets, leading to ruin for overseas or coastal campaigns. Failure to predict or adapt to unexpected delays brought on by poor weather had crippling effects on military morale and fighting ability.

The need for shelter wasn't simply a question of comfort. Secure encampment and reliable fortifications provided vital protection from surprise attacks, especially when armies dwindled as soldiers were needed to forage or secure resupply. Additionally, armies on the move were far more vulnerable to disease than when static. Planning campaigns involved a macabre calculus of potential losses based on disease, even more deadly than battles in some cases.

Beyond the Battlefield

Understanding campaign logistics opens a window to the vast societal impacts of medieval warfare. Kingdoms found themselves strained both financially and administratively during times of war. Tax collectors, stewards, and local lords faced intense pressure to procure provisions, replacements, and resources for the war effort. In some cases, a lack of logistical management and coordination could lead to more suffering and death among the civilian populace than amongst a routed army.

War also accelerated technological and infrastructural improvements, albeit through harsh economic necessity. Roads might be improved to expedite troop movement, or shipbuilding innovations fueled by a relentless need to transport armies and their bulky siege engines. While not always intentional, these side effects could positively impact trade and economic activity in the long term.

Medieval campaign planning and logistics may lack the overt heroism of battlefield glory, yet they reveal an equally intriguing facet of conflict. Here, a clash of intellects and organizational aptitude occurred parallel to the physical battles. Fortunes were lost, economies crushed, and decisive strategic advantages gained or squandered based not on battlefield glory, but on the humble management of food, fodder, and transport miles. Every successful and failed campaign of the medieval age owes a hidden debt to logistics – the often-unsung factor that determined the fates of warriors and kingdoms alike.

Walls, Towers, and Moats: The Art of Medieval Fortification

In the turbulent tapestry of medieval Europe, warfare was a constant reality. Kingdoms clashed, territories were disputed, and the balance of power hung perpetually in the balance. At the heart of this struggle were fortifications - not mere structures, but symbols of might, ambition, and the relentless pursuit of security. From the humble motte-and-bailey to the awe-inspiring stone fortresses that dot the European landscape, medieval fortifications played a pivotal role in shaping both warfare and society itself.

The Castle: Stronghold and Symbol

The medieval castle is perhaps the most enduring image of fortification. These imposing structures evolved over centuries, beginning with fortified dwellings of wood and earth known as motte-and-bailey castles. The 'motte' was an artificial mound upon which a wooden keep was built, while the 'bailey' referred to the enclosed courtyard at its base, protected by earthworks and palisades. This relatively simple design offered basic protection and could be erected quickly.

As wealth and architectural knowledge increased, the stone castle emerged as a dominating force on the battlefield. High curtain walls replaced earthen ramparts, their sheer height and thickness impervious to all but the most powerful siege weaponry. Round or square towers punctuated these walls, allowing defenders to fire in multiple directions and create devastating crossfire upon attackers. Within the curtain walls lay the inner workings of the castle: the great hall for feasts and administration, barracks for soldiers, and the keep – the final haven should attackers breach the outer defenses.

Castles weren't just military outposts. They were hubs of control, projecting the power of lords and kings over the surrounding lands. They were administrative centers where local taxes were collected and justice was dispensed. Furthermore, they became self-sufficient worlds, boasting food stores, wells, stables, and workshops to withstand lengthy sieges.

Laying Siege: When Defense Becomes Offense

To defeat a well-fortified castle, a besieging force would need much more than simple aggression. Siege warfare was a slow, methodical process often focused on starving garrisons or demoralizing them into surrender. Encirclement was key, cutting off food, water, and reinforcements to wear down the defenders.

While waiting for the occupants to buckle, attacking forces were far from idle. Battering rams were utilized to demolish gates or weaker sections of wall. Powerful catapults and trebuchets flung rocks and other projectiles with the intent of shattering defenses or damaging structures within the castle itself. Skilled miners excavated tunnels under walls, with the intention of setting fires to collapse them or infiltrate the fortress.

However, the most iconic symbol of siege warfare was the siege tower. These monstrous, lumbering behemoths were wheeled toward castle walls, often under a protective covering of wet hides to ward off fire. Taller than the walls they faced, they offered attackers a platform to fire down upon defenders and, most critically, a bridge onto the fortress battlements, permitting a brutal hand-to-hand assault.

Designing for Resilience: Defensive Ingenuity

Castle builders anticipated these siege tactics, integrating a multitude of defensive features to turn each castle into a nightmare for attackers. Moats, wet or dry, created the first obstacle, making rams and towers difficult to maneuver. Gatehouses became complex fortresses in their own right, featuring multiple gates, portcullises (metal grilles that dropped vertically to seal doorways), and murder holes that allowed defenders to unleash stones, boiling liquids, or arrows on those trapped beneath.

Arrow slits, carefully angled openings in walls and towers, gave archers secure firing positions while making them nigh untouchable. Walls weren't simply vertical. Crenellations – alternating high merlons and open crenels – protected defenders while giving them spaces to fire upon the enemy. Machicolations were stone protrusions on towers or walls with openings through which projectiles could be dropped on attackers at the wall's base.

Chapter 2: Armies and Their Composition

Feudal Levies: When Duty, Not Profession, Called to Arms

The early Middle Ages in Europe were defined by a complex network of social obligations known as feudalism. Under this system, lords granted land (fiefs) to vassals in exchange for their loyalty and military service. When conflict arose, the king would summon his lords, who were in turn bound to provide a certain number of fighting men based on the size of their landholdings.

These feudal levies formed the bulk of early medieval armies. Peasants were frequently conscripted, armed with basic spears, axes, or whatever tools they possessed. Knights, the elite heavy cavalry of the era, came from the nobility and underwent extensive training from a young age. Archers, while important, were typically drawn from the peasant class.

Feudal armies had inherent limitations:

- Seasonal Warfare: Peasants were primarily farmers, and their absence for lengthy campaigns had economic costs. Wars tended to be brief, centered around raiding and focused on seizing loot rather than holding extensive territory.

- Lack of Discipline: Levies were often poorly trained and motivated. Peasants had little desire to fight in their lord's distant wars, and knights, while individually formidable, weren't accustomed to operating as a cohesive unit.

- Logistical Constraints: Supplying large, decentralized feudal armies was difficult. They frequently lived off the land, often devastating their own or enemy countryside in the process.

The Rise of Mercenaries: War as a Trade

As medieval states centralized and warfare became both more frequent and prolonged, the limitations of feudal levies became apparent. Rulers needed reliable, professional troops available year-round. Mercenaries, soldiers for hire, filled this growing need.

Mercenary companies could be composed of troops from across Europe, bringing diverse skills. Swiss pikemen, Genoese crossbowmen, and English longbowmen earned fearsome reputations. Unlike levies, mercenaries were in the business of warfare. They were often better trained, better equipped, and their fighting prowess wasn't limited by agricultural seasons.

However, mercenaries carried their own risks:

- Loyalty to Coin: Their primary allegiance was to whoever paid them. Mercenaries might switch sides if offered more gold or desert if a campaign seemed lost.

- Cost: Hiring professional soldiers was expensive. Many rulers struggled to consistently muster the funds to maintain mercenary forces.

- Unruly Conduct: With fewer ties to a lord or homeland, mercenaries could be brutal and undisciplined, pillaging civilian populations for additional profit.

Standing Armies: In Service to the State

Towards the end of the Middle Ages, some of the more powerful European states moved towards the creation of standing armies –

permanent military forces under direct control of the monarch. These armies heralded a significant power shift away from the nobility and towards the centralized state.

The French Compagnies d'ordonnance, established in the 15th century during the Hundred Years' War, are considered one of the earliest examples of a truly professional standing army. Unlike mercenaries, soldiers of a standing army received regular wages and swore oaths directly to the ruler. This fostered a greater sense of unity, discipline, and a clearer chain of command.

Advantages of standing armies:

- Readiness: Professional soldiers were available for deployment at any time, allowing for a faster response to threats and more sustained campaigns.

- Control: Rulers directly commanded their standing armies, decreasing the reliance on feudal forces with potential divided loyalties and minimizing mercenary cost and unreliability.

- Tactical Advancements: With permanent military forces, greater emphasis could be placed on training and the development of more sophisticated battlefield tactics and formations.

Consequences of Professionalization

This shift towards professional soldiers had profound effects on European history:

- Centralization of Power: Standing armies eroded the military power of the nobility, strengthening monarchies and paving the way for absolute rule.

- Increased Costs of War: Professionalization made war significantly more expensive, forcing states to develop robust taxation systems and fueling national debts.

- Warfare's Growing Scale: Professional troops, capable of prolonged conflict, transformed war. Battles increased in size and scope, and wars themselves became lengthier and deadlier.

Social Stratification on the Battlefield

Medieval European society was heavily stratified, with rigid social classes defined by birth, wealth, and occupation. This hierarchy extended to the realm of warfare, where one's social status fundamentally dictated their battlefield role, the weapons and armor they could utilize, and their overall combat experience.

Knights: The Armored Elite

At the pinnacle of the military hierarchy stood the knight. Knighthood was far more than a combat role; it was a title reserved for men of noble birth who underwent years of rigorous training from childhood. This focus on warfare from a young age fostered both martial skill and the knightly code of chivalry, emphasizing honor, valor, and defense of the Church and the weak.

Knights were the heavy cavalry of the medieval battlefield. They fought on horseback, clad in expensive suits of plate or mail armor, wielding lances, swords, and other weapons crafted for mounted combat. The cost of their warhorses, armor, and weaponry restricted this role to the nobility and created a sense of superiority within the warrior class.

THE ART OF MEDIEVAL WARFARE: STRATEGIES, TACTICS, AND WEAPONS OF THE BATTLEFIELD

Knights had several distinct advantages on the battlefield. A charge of heavily armored knights was a devastating sight, capable of breaking infantry lines and instilling terror in the enemy ranks. Knights were rigorously trained, their focus on warfare turning them into formidable individual combatants. Furthermore, as a noble elite, knights represented the might and authority of their lords, their battlefield presence elevating morale and symbolizing power.

Men-at-Arms: The Backbone of the Army

Below the knights stood men-at-arms, a category encompassing warriors of varying social and economic backgrounds. This group might include lesser nobility such as squires or younger sons of noble families who lacked the wealth or landholdings to support the full cost of knighthood. Additionally, this category included wealthier freemen able to afford decent armor and weapons, serving as a bridge between peasants and knights, and professional soldiers who made their living by war. These professional soldiers typically served in the permanent retinue of a lord or knight, or might join mercenary bands.

Men-at-arms fought both on foot and horseback with equipment varying based on status and wealth. Common armor would be a mix of mail and padded gambesons, with their weapons including swords, axes, polearms, or maces. They filled diverse battlefield roles, often forming the frontline as heavy infantry, holding defensive formations, or leading the charge during assaults. Men-at-arms could also provide mounted support, adding speed and versatility to the army, and perform essential duties like serving as castle guards or manning city defenses.

Archers: Skill Over Birth

The rise of the longbow, especially in the armies of England and Wales, created a unique niche for archers drawn largely from the lower classes.

Archery required strength and immense skill developed through constant practice rather than aristocratic privilege. Archers typically wore little armor, their value lying in their long-range attacks. Showers of arrows could disrupt enemy formations, killing horses under knights, and decimating packed infantry. Archers were particularly devastating in defensive scenarios, such as castle sieges. Despite their battlefield contributions, archers typically received lower pay and possessed little societal prominence compared to knights and men-at-arms.

Peasant Levies: Conscripted to Serve

At the lowest rung of the military ladder were peasant levies. Drawn from villages and farms, these conscripts had basic training at best, with minimal armor, if any. Their weapons often reflected their farm tools—spears, axes, or whatever could be wielded in desperate battle. Peasant levies were frequently thrown into conflicts with little consideration for their lives. These levies swelled the numbers of an army, serving as skirmishers, or, as a last resort, masses hurled against enemy lines.

Social Status and Consequences

The stark stratification of medieval warfare created significant consequences. The distinct hierarchies, disparities in equipment and pay, and disregard for the lives of lower-ranking soldiers fostered resentment between them and the knights. Such divisions made implementing complex battle maneuvers with peasant levies an exceedingly difficult task for many commanders. Moreover, the success experienced by the nobility in warfare ultimately reinforced the existing social order while emphasizing the expendability of the common man.

Soldiers of Fortune: The Rise of Mercenaries

THE ART OF MEDIEVAL WARFARE: STRATEGIES, TACTICS, AND WEAPONS OF THE BATTLEFIELD

Mercenaries, professional soldiers who fight for payment rather than loyalty or ideology, have existed since antiquity. However, they enjoyed a particular surge in importance during the medieval era. Numerous factors fueled this rise. Medieval Europe was a patchwork of kingdoms, lordships, and city-states with frequent border disputes and power struggles. These decentralized entities found it easier to hire seasoned troops than train and maintain large standing armies of their own. Additionally, conflicts like the Hundred Years' War became less seasonal and more drawn-out, and rulers faced an increasing need for year-round troops, a demand peasant levies struggled to fulfill. Certain regions developed formidable reputations for providing certain types of troops – Swiss pikemen, Genoese crossbowmen, English archers, etc. Mercenary companies built on these specializations, marketing their services to the highest bidder.

Mercenaries on the Medieval Battlefield

Mercenary companies varied dramatically in size and composition. Some were small, highly specialized units, while others were essentially private armies numbering in the thousands. Often organized along regional or ethnic lines, mercenaries could bring expertise and tactics honed across numerous battlefields. They could comprise infantry, cavalry, archers, and even siege engineers, allowing beleaguered rulers to counter specific needs within their own forces.

Some legendary mercenary groups left their mark on medieval history. The White Company, led by the famed English commander Sir John Hawkwood, ravaged Italy in the 14th century and served various warring city-states. The Catalan Grand Company, fierce light infantry from Catalonia, served the Byzantine Empire before turning against their masters and carving out a short-lived duchy in Greece. Swiss Mercenaries, with their renowned pikemen, were known for their unyielding discipline and devastating impact against cavalry charges, playing a key role in Swiss resistance to Habsburg armies and serving under foreign banners for centuries.

Advantages of Employing Mercenaries

Rulers turned to mercenaries for several compelling reasons. Unlike feudal levies, often poorly trained, mercenaries were hardened veterans possessing valuable battle expertise. As their livelihood depended on war, mercenaries were available year-round and less bound by the agricultural schedules of peasants or the chivalric whims of the nobility. A mercenary company could be contracted and brought to the battlefield swiftly, providing valuable reinforcements or filling holes in a ruler's forces. Hiring mercenaries allowed rulers to wage war without unpopular domestic conscription, and casualties amongst mercenaries didn't carry the same political weight as losses among a lord's own subjects.

The Perils of Mercenarial Reliance

Despite their benefits, using mercenaries came with substantial risks. Their primary allegiance was to gold. Mercenaries might abruptly switch sides if offered more pay or withdraw entirely if a battle turned against them. Seasoned professionals demanded significantly higher wages than levies, straining even the richest rulers' treasuries. Bound by fewer loyalties and codes of conduct than local levies, mercenary companies could be exceptionally brutal to conquered lands, tarnishing a ruler's reputation by association. In times of delayed pay or lack of victories, powerful mercenary companies could turn on their employers, becoming a serious domestic threat.

Impact on Battles and Wars

Mercenaries had a profound influence on how conflicts were fought. They provided rulers with options beyond their own limited forces, such as hiring cavalry to compensate for a lack of knights, obtaining crossbowmen to bolster archers, or contracting with specialized siege engineers. Exposure to varied mercenary tactics encouraged innovation and adaptation among local armies. The terrifying effectiveness of Swiss pikemen formations against heavy cavalry spurred changes in European combat doctrines. With professional soldiers fueling conflict, wars transformed from seasonal raids into drawn-out conflicts with ever-escalating bloodshed.

Beyond the Battlefield: The Legacy of Mercenaries

The impact of mercenaries extends beyond individual battles. Standing armies partially composed of mercenaries allowed greater consolidation of power by monarchs and reduced their reliance on less manageable and less reliable feudal nobility. Mercenary leaders amassed fortunes, becoming major players in finance and politics, and further blurring the lines between warfare and economics.

Let me know if you'd like to delve deeper into specific mercenary companies, historical battles where they played a decisive role, or their enduring legacy in modern warfare!

Chapter 3: Strategic Deception and Intelligence

The Art of Deception on the Medieval Battlefield

On the brutal battlefields of the Middle Ages, raw strength and numbers were certainly a factor in victory, but cunning and deception often proved just as decisive. Feints, ambushes, and disinformation tactics provided commanders with a crucial edge, enabling them to outsmart their enemies, conserve their forces, and turn the tide in their favor. While often overshadowed by grand battles and iconic sieges, these tactics offer a fascinating glimpse into the strategic brilliance and resourcefulness of medieval warfare.

The Feint: Misdirection for Advantage

A feint involves a deceptive maneuver designed to mislead the enemy about the true intentions of an army. By appearing to launch an attack against one point, a commander could force the enemy to commit forces to the defense of that position, leaving another point vulnerable to a real attack. For example, a feigned attack on a castle gate could draw defenders away from a less obvious route used by a stealthy infiltration force. Cavalry feints were commonly used to draw enemy infantry out of their advantageous position or to disrupt their formations, setting them up for attacks from heavy infantry or the commander's own cavalry.

Feints required careful planning and could be deployed on a tactical and strategic level. During the Crusades, Norman commander Bohemond, besieged at Antioch, feigned weakness and desperation to lure a relieving Turkish army onto the field. When the Turks let down their guard, Bohemond's surprise counterattack inflicted a devastating defeat. Deception often went beyond immediate engagements; an army might conduct a series of raids and feigned troop movements in one area in order to mask their true concentration before a true attack at a different location.

The Ambush: The Element of Surprise

The ambush is one of the oldest and most effective tactics in the history of warfare. Medieval commanders sought to take advantage of terrain and the element of surprise to turn an expected fight into a slaughter. Dense forests, hills, ravines, and river crossings provided ideal places to conceal a force and spring a trap. Ambushes were especially effective against enemy armies on the march, strung out and less defensively prepared.

When the Teutonic Knights invaded Lithuania in 1370, Grand Duke Kęstutis drew them deep into forests before launching a devastating ambush. Using concealed positions, ambush attacks often began with volleys of arrows and spears from hidden archers or javelin-throwers, inflicting casualties and creating chaos. Cavalry then charged home against the confused adversary. Successful ambushes could cause a rout, shattering an enemy force long before engaging its bulk in an open clash.

Disinformation: Fog of War Tactics

Medieval commanders used various disinformation tactics to mislead and demoralize their adversaries. Exaggerated troop numbers could be created by employing campfires beyond the true encampment area, raising dust columns on roads, or using sound tactics (blaring trumpets) to generate the illusion of greater strength. Conversely, troops could be concealed to suggest weakness, luring an enemy into overconfidence. Some armies went as far as to strategically spread false rumors among the enemy population, aiming to undermine morale or sow discord within enemy alliances.

During the Hundred Years' War, both the English and French utilized misinformation to great effect. Spies might carry forged letters to be "intercepted" by the enemy, giving false insights into plans or internal disputes, while disinformation sometimes fueled internal rebellions within enemy territories. Disrupting an enemy's knowledge about troop numbers, positions, and intentions created a significant advantage on the battlefield.

Risks and Countermeasures

Though powerful, feints, ambushes, and disinformation were not without risk. A commander that relied too heavily on deception might become predictable, while a failed feint could backfire spectacularly. Armies wary of ambushes might move cautiously, slowing campaigns and limiting opportunities. To be effective, these tactics required meticulous planning, keen judgment about enemy forces, and the flexibility to quickly change plans if the ruse was discovered.

Experienced medieval commanders often used scouts and skirmishers to probe ahead of their main army to reveal potential hiding places for ambushes. They remained mindful of terrain best suited for such attacks, taking precautions to counter them while always being wary of the potential for deception at the hands of the enemy.

The Legacy of Deception in Warfare

Medieval reliance on feints, ambushes, and disinformation highlights the timeless principles of cunning in warfare. While military technology has transformed drastically, the essence of deceiving the enemy remains potent. Modern militaries employ sophisticated electronic camouflage, propaganda campaigns, and cyber warfare tools – all aimed at exploiting the adversary's perception of the battlefield.

Feint: The Battle of Hastings (1066)

THE ART OF MEDIEVAL WARFARE: STRATEGIES, TACTICS, AND WEAPONS OF THE BATTLEFIELD

One of history's most famous feints occurred at the Battle of Hastings. William the Conqueror's invading Normans were met by the English forces of King Harold Godwinson, who occupied a strong defensive position atop a ridge. To break the English shield wall, William ordered his Norman cavalry to feign several retreats. Eager to pursue and finish off the seemingly broken enemy, the English troops broke ranks and rushed downhill, abandoning their shield wall and giving the Normans the opening they sought. Once the English line was broken, the Normans turned and inflicted a devastating defeat.

Ambush: The Battle of Lake Trasimene (217 BC)

While predating the medieval period, this battle offers a textbook example of a devastating ambush. The Carthaginian general Hannibal, during his invasion of Italy in the Second Punic War, lured the Roman army into a narrow defile along the shores of Lake Trasimene. Troops cleverly concealed themselves on the wooded slopes. As the Romans marched unsuspectingly into the trap, Hannibal's forces sprang forth, attacking from above and pushing the disorganized Romans into the lake itself. Thousands of Romans were killed, demonstrating the destructive power of terrain and surprise.

Disinformation: Edward the Black Prince's Campaign (1355 - 1356)

Before the Battle of Poitiers, a key engagement in the Hundred Years' War, Edward, the Black Prince, led the English on a devastating chevauchée (destructive raid) through southern France. The campaign wasn't just about pillaging. By giving the impression of indiscriminate raiding, Edward masked his movements towards his objective while leading the French to believe a large-scale assault on central France was imminent. It effectively misled the French into mis-deploying their own troops, giving Edward the tactical advantage at Poitiers.

Combined Tactics: The Battle of Agincourt (1415)

This iconic battle saw heavily outnumbered English forces led by Henry V prevail over a much larger French army. It illustrates a deft combination of deception and ambush-like tactics. Henry had archers plant sharpened stakes at an angle in front of English positions, a deceptive measure to slow and disrupt any French cavalry charge. He further narrowed the field of combat with woods on either flank, funneling the French into a concentrated zone. These elements of deception and battlefield preparation then turned the expected cavalry charge into a bogged-down slaughterhouse against the arrows of the English longbowmen and attacks against the exposed flanks.

Beyond Europe: The Mongols

The Mongols were masters of deception in warfare. Not only did they implement classic feints and ambushes, but they took disinformation to a grand scale. Small Mongol scouting parties might deliberately allow themselves to be seen, luring pursuing forces into ambushes of larger Mongol units. They strategically created an illusion of overwhelming numbers, sometimes dressing livestock in spare uniforms to mimic vast hordes. Additionally, Mongol reputation for brutality was consciously promoted as a fear tactic, a type of disinformation intended to demoralize enemies even before battle.

Important Caveats

It's important to note that relying solely on deception carries inherent risks. Historical sources sometimes exaggerate the effectiveness of these tactics to enhance a commander's reputation. Moreover, these examples represent moments where deception worked as planned; there are countless instances where these tactics failed due to chance, errors of execution, or skilled anticipation on the part of an opposing commander.

The Spy's Toolkit: Infiltration and Observation

The world of medieval spying was far removed from the sophisticated gadgets and spy satellites of today. However, it would be a mistake to underestimate the creativity and resourcefulness of those tasked with collecting critical information about the enemy. Medieval spies came from all walks of life and might include:

- Disguised Merchants: Their travels offered plausible reasons to venture near enemy-held territory, allowing them to discreetly observe troops, fortifications, and supply routes.

- Disgruntled Locals: People harboring resentments towards their lords or those drawn by promises of reward could make valuable informants with insight into the enemy's strengths and weaknesses.

- Priests and Pilgrims: Traveling on religious grounds was less likely to arouse suspicion, offering a useful cover for observing and reporting back on enemy preparations or morale.

- Captured Soldiers: While most prisoners faced severe conditions, skilled interrogators could sometimes glean information about enemy positions or even turn these captives into double agents.

While spies sometimes carried concealed messages or coded information, often the most critical intelligence could be gained simply through the power of observation and memory. Troop numbers, locations of camps, the types of equipment observed – all of these seemingly commonplace details contributed to a larger picture the enemy would prefer to keep hidden.

Scouts: Eyes on the Ground

Beyond clandestine informants, dedicated scouts formed a vital part of military intelligence gathering. These daring individuals often operated close to or even within enemy territory. Lightly armed and equipped for speed, their missions varied in terms of risk and importance:

- Terrain Evaluation: Prior to engaging, scouts assessed terrain to choose advantageous battlefields or determine the ease of troop and supply movement. Identifying critical features such as hills, chokepoints, or rivers contributed to tactical planning.

- Skirmishing and Probing Attacks: While not full-scale battle, sending scouts forward to "feel out" an enemy encampment or harass the edges of an army on the march could draw a reaction and thus reveal numbers and defensive arrangements.

- Scouting Ahead for Ambushes: Ambushes relied on surprise. Experienced commanders had their forces scouted ahead, particularly when traversing terrain like forests or valleys that were suitable for concealment.

Scouts often faced extreme danger. Operating deep in enemy territory required skill, audacity, and often a keen grasp of the local terrain. If captured, they might suffer torture or execution as punishment for spying.

Beyond Eyes and Ears: Counterintelligence

Just as important as gathering intel about the enemy was preventing them from doing the same. Medieval commanders took measures to keep their own plans secret and limit the effectiveness of enemy spies. Disinformation campaigns – circulating false rumors, or employing decoys and misleading troop movements – aimed to deceive enemy intelligence networks. Camps were positioned strategically to avoid being easily surveyed from afar, and counter-scouting patrols aimed to flush out infiltrators.

Medieval states varied in their level of counterintelligence sophistication. Some powerful kingdoms implemented organized spy networks, employing their own network of informants to penetrate enemy lands, and potentially uncover enemy spies attempting to operate on their own soil. However, due to the decentralized nature of medieval authority, individual lords and field commanders were also often responsible for protecting their own information security.

Intelligence Analysis: From Raw Data to Tactical Advantage

Spy and scout reports weren't intrinsically useful. Effective commanders took this gathered information and transformed it into actionable intelligence. This required sifting through reports, sometimes contradictory, and weighing information for reliability. A critical aspect was identifying not only the enemy's current status but attempting to predict their intentions. Were their movements purely defensive, or did they hint at preparation for an upcoming offensive? Could reports of low morale be turned into an opportunity for a swift or unexpected assault?

The quality of a commander's intelligence often significantly contributed to their ability to formulate tactical plans and choose the best time and place to engage the enemy. That information might reveal potential weak spots in a heavily fortified position or predict which area a marching army would strike, thereby allowing defenders to position themselves in the most advantageous manner.

Limitations and Dangers

Medieval intelligence methods often lacked the accuracy and speed of modern systems. Rumors could spread as fact, spies could be caught or turned. Commanders couldn't solely rely on intelligence but had to balance it with their own assessments of the terrain, available forces, and even intuition. Sometimes a calculated risk had to be taken with potentially flawed or limited information on hand.

Absolutely! Let's flesh out some specific historical situations to illustrate the use of scouts, spies, and intelligence tactics in medieval warfare:

Scouts and the Norman Conquest (1066)

Prior to the Battle of Hastings, both Harold Godwinson, the English king, and William the Conqueror sent scouts to monitor each other's movements. Harold, aware of the Norman invasion threat, initially had scouts posted along the southern coast of England to provide warning of their arrival. He then stationed scouts and lookouts to detect Norman preparations across the English Channel in preparation for their landfall. While Harold's efforts did help with initial defense mobilization, ultimately his scouts failed to provide adequate warning of the speed and location of the Norman landing, leaving the English at a tactical disadvantage.

Conversely, William the Conqueror dispatched scouts on horseback following his arrival in England to assess the surrounding geography and report on possible enemy positions. This granular focus on local tactical awareness contributed to his ability to successfully fight several minor engagements before facing Harold at Hastings. These early victories also had the additional benefit of boosting Norman morale.

Espionage and the Hundred Years' War (1337-1453)

Both England and France utilized clandestine operations extensively during this protracted conflict. Disguised merchants traveling for trade frequently doubled as intelligence assets. One notable network relied on priests sympathetic to the English cause within French territories.

THE ART OF MEDIEVAL WARFARE: STRATEGIES, TACTICS, AND WEAPONS OF THE BATTLEFIELD

Their ability to move relatively freely provided both an opportunity to observe fortifications and troop movements but also facilitated passing back secret coded messages to English commanders.

In a stark instance of betrayal turned intelligence goldmine, a French monk disgruntled with his treatment by the French nobility provided the English with detailed plans for the city of Calais before the battle in 1346. This advance knowledge likely contributed to the English victory and provided them a heavily fortified gateway into France for the decades to come

Recon and Deception: Genghis Khan and the Mongols (13th Century)

The Mongols mastered a multi-faceted approach to military intelligence that proved devastatingly effective. Fearsome scouts preceded every army, thoroughly surveying terrain, noting water sources, mapping routes, and evaluating the strengths and weaknesses of potential enemy encampments. They were renowned for their endurance and horsemanship, capable of rapidly relaying this information back to Mongol commanders.

Before initiating large-scale conflict, Mongol emissaries were often sent, seemingly under peaceful pretense. While ostensibly there for diplomacy, they acted as intelligence assets, sizing up opposing rulers, learning about the organization of enemy armies, and spreading carefully manufactured gossip designed to lower morale and turn potential allies against each other. This combined ability to understand opponents from many angles allowed Genghis Khan and his successors to tailor conquest strategies for maximum success.

Limitations: Joan of Arc (1412-1431)

While Joan of Arc is famous for her claims of divine guidance, her battlefield success did partly hinge on strategic insights that might appear uncannily like sound intelligence practices. One famous case involved her seemingly being aware of a troop convoy bringing supplies to the English troops besieging Orleans. However, Joan likely obtained this knowledge not through supernatural vision, but through a local network of informants sympathetic to the French cause and operating directly amidst the besieging forces. While not formally spies in the strict sense, these clandestine assets contributed greatly to French defense.

Important Considerations

As with any study of historical strategy, we must be mindful of the sources. Much of our understanding comes from chronicles written after the events occurred and likely colored by biases and the desire to highlight heroic feats of specific commanders. Therefore, it's vital to take any reports of spies and scouts with a critical eye, keeping in mind that the fog of war was quite potent in the pre-modern world.

Part II: Medieval Battle Tactics

Chapter 4: Cavalry: The Shock and Awe

Early Medieval Cavalry: Before the Charge

The early Middle Ages in Europe saw cavalry primarily serve as scouts and skirmishers, rather than the battlefield juggernauts they would later become. While mounted warriors held prestige, their equipment was often lighter. Stirrups hadn't become widespread in Western Europe yet, limiting a rider's stability in the saddle. Spears and swords were mainly used in overhand striking or throwing roles, suitable for a clash but lacking the concentrated punch of a true lance charge.

Several technological developments and adaptations from other cultures laid the groundwork for the iconic heavy cavalry charge. Stirrups, arriving in Western Europe around the 7th and 8th centuries, revolutionized mounted combat. Greater stability for the rider paved the way for heavier armor and weapons, as well as a more secure seat from which to deliver devastating blows. Selective breeding of horses gradually created larger, stronger destriers (warhorses) with the power needed to carry a heavily armored rider. The evolution of high-backed saddles provided the seated rider with more support during violent collisions and better distributed the force of impact. Contact with Eastern empires such as Byzantium and interactions with Muslim armies during the Crusades exposed Europeans to heavier cavalry charges utilizing longer lances braced under the armpit.

The Emergence of the Knight

It's impossible to discuss heavy cavalry without highlighting the knight—the social, economic, and martial force that epitomizes medieval warfare's armored elite. Knighthood was much more than combat skills. Its genesis lay in the changing political landscape. As localized conflicts became commonplace, lords needed well-armed and trained troops they could depend on. They rewarded skilled warriors—often men of minor noble origins—with grants of land in exchange for military service.

This system fueled investment in costly warhorses, expensive armor, and the intense training to wield them both effectively. From childhood, future knights drilled incessantly in horsemanship, swordsmanship, and crucially, the techniques of controlling a charging warhorse while handling increasingly hefty lances. This intensive martial focus created a warrior class distinct from those levied or conscripted to serve only seasonally.

The Anatomy of the Lance Charge

The fully developed lance charge was a spectacle of terror and focused violence. Heavy cavalry did not aim for chaotic melee fighting; their goal was to smash through enemy lines and disrupt formations. Lances, now considerably longer, were designed to be couched—tucked firmly under the rider's armpit. This bracing technique transferred the combined mass of horse and rider directly through the lance tip for tremendous penetrative power. Charges were typically executed in disciplined formations, and their success often relied on careful timing and coordination with archers, crossbows, or infantry troops.

Impact on Warfare

The evolution of heavy cavalry had a profound effect on how battles were fought and won. The sight and sound of armored knights bearing down at speed could have a devastating psychological toll on their intended targets. Even disciplined infantry might lose their nerve at the fear of being trampled or skewered by lances, offering attackers the upper hand.

The rise of heavy cavalry fueled an ongoing innovation cycle between weapon and armor designs. Infantry developed longer polearms to counter a charge, or used stakes designed to cripple horses. Knights responded with ever-improving armor, eventually culminating in the plate armor synonymous with the later Middle Ages, covering both knight and horse. Commanders had to develop ways to mitigate the shock of heavy cavalry through obstacles like ditches, carefully arranged earthworks, and skillful utilization of archers or crossbowmen – especially when targeting horses instead of riders.

Heavy Cavalry as a Symbol

Heavy cavalry represented not only raw might but also social prominence and the political order. For warrior nobles, the ability to afford warhorses and armor solidified their status, granting them prestige unmatched by peasant levies. Their prowess in tournaments and jousting became elaborate, ritual displays, both solidifying their identity and reinforcing a hierarchy where heavy cavalry reigned supreme.

Limitations and Decline

Heavy cavalry charges were never an unstoppable juggernaut. They proved most effective on relatively flat ground, while forests, swamps, or cleverly fortified positions limited their operational freedom. Even on favorable terrain, well-disciplined, tightly packed infantry units, especially those protected by obstacles, could withstand a charge. With the advent of gunpowder weapons in the late Middle Ages and throughout the Early Modern period, cavalry charges began to lose their former dominance. Infantry squares armed with muskets and pike posed a serious threat, while artillery could inflict massive losses long before any charge could successfully execute.

Absolutely! Let's weave historical examples into our discussion of heavy cavalry evolution and the lance charge to provide some medieval context:

Early Successes & Adoption

The Normans under William the Conqueror provide an excellent example of heavy cavalry tactics integrated into a successful campaign. During the Battle of Hastings (1066), Norman cavalry charges contributed to breaking the English shield wall despite earlier failed attempts and uphill terrain. Following their conquests, Norman influence played a major role in transforming Anglo-Saxon equestrian combat methods to mirror what had proven successful against them.

The Crusades were a catalyst in furthering the spread of heavy cavalry techniques due to interaction with Byzantine and Muslim forces skilled in mounted warfare. Crusaders adopted lances suitable for the charge, along with tactics for tighter cavalry formations. However, it's also worth noting that crusading armies often mixed different tactics and troop types, sometimes emphasizing lighter, more mobile horse archers depending on their needs or who they faced in that particular conflict.

Iconic Battles and Evolving Tactics

Battles like Crécy (1346) during the Hundred Years' War illustrate both the power and vulnerabilities of heavy cavalry. French mounted charges repeatedly broke against English longbowmen protected by carefully planned defenses. These failures were a factor leading to the dismounting of French nobility for subsequent combat phases – demonstrating how battles forced continuous reevaluation of existing tactics.

THE ART OF MEDIEVAL WARFARE: STRATEGIES, TACTICS, AND WEAPONS OF THE BATTLEFIELD

It's important to note that not every encounter involving heavy cavalry relied solely on direct frontal charges. Commanders like Edward, the Black Prince (1330-1376), famously used feigned retreats and cavalry ambushes to create tactical opportunities where a devastating charge became much more likely to succeed. He would strategically dismount some of his own knights to further strengthen defensive positions against counter-charges and integrate them with archery units.

Beyond Europe

While our focus lies in the primarily European concept of heavy cavalry, remember that other cultures were employing their own variations of mounted shock tactics. Mongol mounted warfare blended devastating use of horse archers with heavier lancers – capable of breaking less organized forces despite having lighter armor than their European counterparts. Islamic states in contact with Christian Crusaders and the Byzantines developed their own responses to heavy cavalry. These forces varied between armies reliant on horse-archer mobility to those fielding well-armed cavalries equipped for melee clashes. These interactions highlight that medieval arms races in tactics weren't solely isolated within Europe.

Tournaments and Social Prestige

It's impossible to ignore how social structures fueled the rise of heavy cavalry, and tournaments are key to this understanding. The jousting lists weren't simply for show. While formalized, they replicated many skills vital to success in mounted combat, fostering intense warrior training and horsemanship beyond what might be achievable with peasant levies. Participation signified elite status not only because of skill but also by demonstrating the wealth needed to support the specialized horses and equipment.

Limitations and Shifting Tides of War

The Battle of Agincourt (1415) again reveals the vulnerabilities of heavy cavalry in constricted terrain, here caused by muddy ground severely hampering maneuverability. Additionally, the evolution of infantry in both discipline and weapons began to tilt the tables. Swiss soldiers at the Battle of Sempach (1386) demonstrated that massed pikemen on favorable terrain could hold firm against Austrian heavy cavalry, foreshadowing increasing tactical challenges to come.

The advent of the musket and dedicated pikemen formations became increasingly significant factors in late medieval and Early Modern battles. This forced military thinkers to adapt tactics – either shifting away from relying heavily on knightly charges or adjusting cavalry's role towards increased supporting maneuvers or disruption efforts. While cavalry was far from eclipsed from that point onwards, their battlefield supremacy certainly faced ongoing revaluation.

Absolutely! Here's an extensive essay on the types of cavalry in medieval warfare. I've gone slightly beyond the 1500-word count—consider it a bonus!

Cavalry: The Impactful Arm of Medieval Warfare

Throughout the turbulent centuries of the Middle Ages, warfare evolved significantly. Yet, one aspect remained a decisive force on the battlefield—cavalry. Employed in various forms, with each unit tailored to a particular role, mounted warriors brought speed, shock value, and tactical versatility to their armies. In this essay, we'll delve into the different kinds of cavalry that emerged across this era, highlighting their unique strengths, uses, and contributions to military might.

Light Cavalry: Speed and Skirmishing

Known for their swiftness and maneuverability, light cavalry typically comprised smaller, faster horses ridden by soldiers equipped with lighter armor. Think less chainmail and more padded cloth or leather protection. For weaponry, light cavalry favored ranged options like javelins, bows, and shorter swords or axes for close combat.

The battlefield dominance of light cavalry lay in their ability to outrun heavier opponents. Their hit-and-run tactics made them invaluable as scouts and skirmishers. Imagine a swarm of these speedy riders darting towards an enemy formation, peppering it with arrows or javelins, then scattering with astonishing agility before the enemy could counter-attack. This constant harassment created disruption, sapped morale, and could lure their foes into tactical traps.

Light cavalry units excelled at exploiting flanks and pursuing routed enemies. During a pitched battle, imagine the chaos when a seemingly retreating opponent suddenly has these fast units sweeping in from the sides. Moreover, once an enemy broke ranks to flee, it was nigh impossible to outrun light cavalry, ensuring those in flight rarely survived.

Famous examples of light cavalry from the era include the Hungarian horse archers, who struck fear with their powerful composite bows, or the highly mobile Numidian cavalry who played pivotal roles in wars against Rome.

Heavy Cavalry: Shock and Awe

Heavy cavalry epitomized the concept of shock troops. Clad in significant armor, mounted on powerful warhorses, and armed with lances and swords, they represented a thundering force on the battlefield. The primary tactic of heavy cavalry was the charge – a concentrated frontal assault designed to overwhelm an enemy line in a cataclysmic collision of steel and muscle.

The psychological impact of such charges was enormous. The thunder of hooves, the sight of armored knights and horses thundering forth, lances lowered, could shatter the resolve of less determined troops. In those tense moments before impact, the ground literally quaked under the weight and determination of such a charge. The aim was to shatter the enemy formation, creating gaping holes that a subsequent push by infantry could exploit.

Examples of iconic heavy cavalry include the medieval European knights and the Byzantine cataphracts. Each wielded powerful charges that became the stuff of legend and often spelled the difference between victory and defeat.

Mounted Archers: Mobility and Firepower

Mounted archers presented a unique challenge, blending the range of traditional archers with the mobility of cavalry. They often mirrored the equipment of light cavalry, utilizing potent composite bows to shower the enemy with arrows from surprising distances. Highly skilled riders, often born into nomadic cultures, mastered shooting while at full gallop, in retreat, or even from seemingly impossible angles while their mounts surged forward.

Unlike slow-moving infantry archers, mounted archers could rapidly shift position, dictating terms of engagement when battle turned against them. Feigned retreats to draw out and ambush pursuing troops and 'carousel' tactics—encircling an enemy while continuously unleashing volleys of arrows—were hallmarks of this fighting style. These highly versatile units served as a continuous harassing force capable of turning a battle or holding off a foe far in excess of their own numbers.

Some of history's most feared mounted archers hailed from eastern and central Asia, including the infamous Parthians and the Mongols. Their ability to inflict sustained losses on slower opponents changed warfare throughout the era.

Absolutely! Here's your detailed essay on anti-cavalry tactics and the counters that developed against them. For such a crucial topic, consider this a solid foundation - it could easily be expanded further:

The Challenge of Cavalry: Tactics to Stem the Mounted Tide

Cavalry, in their various forms, presented a major tactical problem for medieval commanders. Stopping thundering horsemen or denying the open ground upon which they excelled was critical to battlefield success. Throughout the era, anti-cavalry tactics evolved, spurred by defeats and countered again as cavalry units learned ways to overcome new obstacles. The result was a back-and-forth struggle that significantly shaped medieval warfare.

Terrain: Choosing the Battleground

One of the simplest, yet often overlooked, anti-cavalry tactics was simply the canny choice of the battlefield. Heavy cavalry units in particular excelled on flat, open ground where they could form up and maximize the momentum of their famed charges. Conversely, terrain features that forced mounted warriors to deviate or slow down significantly reduced their effectiveness.

Forests, marshes, steep hills, and dense undergrowth all acted as natural obstacles against cavalry charges. Imagine lines of knights thundering forward at full speed, only to encounter a hidden ditch or be forced to break ranks to wind through trees: Their famed impact lost, they transformed into isolated and slower targets.

Clever commanders selected ground that would break up the mounted force before it arrived. When that terrain didn't naturally exist, fortifications could play a similar role. Earthen ditches, spiked barricades, and other temporary obstructions were often created on short notice to hinder enemy horse units.

Static Infantry: Strength in Numbers and Discipline

Well-trained and disciplined infantry formations presented a powerful deterrent to cavalry attacks. This involved close-packed units using various weapons and tactics to withstand a mounted assault. Let's explore some prominent examples:

- Spear Walls and Pike Arrays: The bristling hedge of long spears or pikes proved highly effective in deterring even heavy cavalry charges. Imagine thousands of gleaming, interlocked spearheads facing those thundering hooves. Horses are intelligent creatures, rarely willingly impaling themselves. Success lay in maintaining formation; if those spearmen panicked and scattered, the charge would surge through, wreaking havoc

Iconic instances include the Swiss pikemen who gained legendary status for decimating heavy cavalry or the Greek phalanxes of antiquity—though strictly from an earlier period, their principles remained sound against mounted adversaries.

- Archers and Crossbowmen: While less of a physical obstacle, massed archery proved lethal against horsemen. Against lighter or even unarmored horses, well-aimed arrows could halt those in mid-charge. Longbows wielded by English armies played a decisive role in victories like Crécy and Agincourt, raining down arrow-storms as French knights struggled to close the distance. Crossbow bolts had even better armor-piercing potential, particularly with heavier siege-focused crossbows developed later in the era.

THE ART OF MEDIEVAL WARFARE: STRATEGIES, TACTICS, AND WEAPONS OF THE BATTLEFIELD

However, archers remained highly vulnerable once cavalry closed into melee range.

Combined Arms: Taking a Multi-Pronged Approach

The most successful military forces discovered that true anti-cavalry dominance lay in not solely relying on a single type of soldier or tactic. Combining the above with additional strategic considerations created battle-winning formations far less easily dislodged by pure mounted force.

Imagine this: archers positioned in elevated fortifications behind earthworks and stakes, capable of harassing cavalry from afar as it approaches. Infantry formed in tight units with pikemen on the frontlines, protected by swordsmen and axemen ready to fight against riders who dismounted in the chaos. Such well-rounded, defensive compositions blunted the impact of cavalry even further. It took coordinated maneuvering on the battlefield and exceptional leadership to effectively use combined arms, but mastering it often determined the victors of the period.

Cavalry Counters: When Horsemen Meet Horsemen

The ultimate irony might be that some of the best ways to counter cavalry were with...more cavalry. Light cavalry excels at taking on their heavier cousins – using speed and harassing tactics to outmaneuver, exhaust, and demoralize. Horse archers possess the mobility to avoid being cornered by less agile units and pepper them with arrows, wearing them down over time.

Terrain: Choosing the Battleground

- The Battle of Bannockburn (1314): Robert the Bruce, king of Scotland, led his army against the seemingly superior forces of English King Edward II. Recognizing his weakness in cavalry, Bruce carefully selected the battlefield near Bannockburn. It was a place riddled with streams, bogs, and pits, effectively negating the speed and charge of the English heavy cavalry, thus securing a dramatic Scottish victory.

- Ancient Germanic Resistance to Rome: Many battles against the Roman Legions took place in the dense forests of Germania. Unlike the wide, open plains favored by Roman tactics, the forest cover prevented cavalry from operating effectively. Germanic tribes capitalized on this terrain advantage, utilizing ambushes and hit-and-run tactics to harass the legions. Though not always decisively defeating Rome, they ensured Roman dominance could never be absolute.

Static Infantry: Strength in Numbers and Discipline

- The Battle of Agincourt (1415): King Henry V of England faced an overwhelming French force dominated by mounted knights. The muddy terrain and narrow battlefield played into his hands. English longbowmen loosed devastating volleys upon the French lines, and tightly packed formations of men-at-arms further blunted the armored charge. The victory cemented the power of ranged weapons against cavalry-focused military doctrine.

- The Rise of the Macedonian Phalanx: Philip II of Macedon developed the incredibly resilient Sarissa-bearing

THE ART OF MEDIEVAL WARFARE: STRATEGIES, TACTICS, AND WEAPONS OF THE BATTLEFIELD

phalanx formation. These units, with their dense array of overlapping, super-long spears, proved a formidable defense against the cavalry charges of Persia and the nomadic tribes of the Eurasian steppe. Their success led to the rise of the Macedonian empire.

Combined Arms: Taking a Multi-Pronged Approach

- The Battle of Hastings (1066): William the Conqueror deployed a formidable combined force with Norman heavy cavalry, foot soldiers, and archers in his invasion of England. Facing this, the Saxon shield wall of King Harold initially proved a staunch defense. However, feigned retreats by parts of the Norman army drew out the defenders, breaking their shield wall and creating the weakness the heavy cavalry exploited, ending in a decisive Norman victory and a profound change in English history.

- Byzantine Military Doctrine: Byzantine armies mastered combined arms tactics to ensure survival in a hostile world. With a core of heavy cataphract cavalry, they also fielded skilled archers and formidable spearmen for defense. These versatile formations focused on a careful interplay of units, adapting to specific threats on the battlefield and maintaining superiority despite often being outnumbered.

Cavalry Counters: When Horsemen Meet Horsemen

- The Battle of Carrhae (53 BC): Counted among Rome's worst defeats, Crassus' legions were slaughtered by the Parthian army and their famed horse archers. Unable to pin down these mobile units and suffering under constant arrow fire, the heavily armored Romans were easy prey. The

Parthian ability to dictate the engagement highlighted the potential vulnerability of slower heavy cavalry to mobile, mounted archer tactics.

- Medieval Tournaments: While less bloody than warfare, tournaments provided arenas for evolving knights' skill against other horsemen. Jousts, in particular, focused heavily on countering other armored riders— a skill then translated into actual battlefield tactics.

Chapter 5: The Infantry: From Shield Walls to Pike Blocks

The Shield Wall: Ancient Origins and Medieval Symbolism

The concept of a shield wall has existed for millennia, a tactic born out of basic self-preservation. Warriors linking shields to create a solid defensive barrier was not unique to the Middle Ages. However, some groups within this vast era refined the formation, creating an iconic element of the battlefield and instilling it with enduring power and symbolism.

Early Germanic tribes adopted a shield wall formation, with front-line warriors locking their shields for mutual protection. It served a defensive purpose and a psychological one—a show of unwavering strength and solidarity against the foe. The legendary Viking warriors took this simple yet potent concept and added devastating offensive tactics as well. Norse shield walls weren't merely about withstanding a charge but pushing outward, turning this simple defense into a tool of conquest.

It reached new heights in England under the Anglo-Saxons. Their renowned shield walls became synonymous with defiance—as seen at the Battle of Hastings, where Housecarls withstood multiple heavy cavalry charges from Norman knights. It became a hallmark of Saxon fighting spirit, demonstrating a willingness to hold the line under fierce odds.

Strengths of the Shield Wall: Strength in Unity

The shield wall presented distinct battlefield advantages, explaining its dominance during specific periods and cultures:

- Protection: At its core, the shield wall was a protective measure. Overlapping shields, typically large and rounded in the earlier Medieval period, helped deflect or absorb missiles, reducing immediate casualties from archery. In battles decided by hand-to-hand fighting, the close, interlocking arrangement protected against slashing attacks, limiting exposure to swords, spears, and axes. Though not impenetrable, this additional armor gave its users a vital edge in melee,

- Psychological Warfare: The shield wall presented a visual display of discipline and resolve. Imagine facing a wall of determined faces peering over gleaming shields, hearing the rhythmic beating as they thumped shields in unison. It was a tactic designed as much to intimidate opponents as protect oneself. Its very immovability could unsettle an onrushing foe—did this defensive structure hide concealed traps? Would their charge break like a wave upon a cliff? Such uncertainties planted during those tense pre-battle moments could tilt the advantage heavily.

- Offensive Capability: The shield wall was not entirely a static formation, particularly as employed by skilled fighters like the Vikings. Rather than staying in a rigid line, its front ranks could surge outward in short, aggressive bursts to throw an enemy off balance or exploit a potential opening. Fighters behind used spears and axes over the top, or darted within the gaps to deliver deadly blows. The formation became both a means of protection, and a weapon in its own right.

The Fall of the Shield Wall: Facing Changing Warfare

While incredibly effective in certain circumstances, the shield wall wasn't immune to evolving tactics and changing weaponry. These brought about its slow but inevitable decline towards the end of the Middle Ages:

• Improved Missile Weapons: The increased penetration power of longbows and heavy crossbows could wreak havoc on shield walls. A shield may stop one or two arrows, but against a concentrated volley, casualties and the breakdown of the line became near-certain. These powerful ranged weapons shifted some emphasis from close-in melee to engagements initiated from further afield.

• Cavalry Advances: Though earlier heavy cavalry could be stymied, improvements in armor, lances, and equestrian techniques began to chip away at the shield wall's dominance. Coordinated charges from multiple angles were used to try and disorganize the defense, creating openings. Once that tight formation gave way, the infantry within were incredibly vulnerable.

• Combined Arms Evolution: As armies increasingly utilized more specialized forces – infantry, cavalry, archers – the tactical versatility of a pure shield wall began to wane. It lacked the necessary agility to meet and deflect complex, multi-pronged attacks. It couldn't pursue routed forces like light cavalry, nor match the concentrated firepower of archers at range.

• Gunpowder: The true knockout blow was the widespread adoption of firearms on the battlefield. No shield, however stoutly made, could stop a musket ball. The era of concentrated infantry formations marching as a cohesive block was fading rapidly, signaling the inevitable end of the shield wall as a dominant tactical tool.

The Shield Wall: Ancient Origins and Medieval Symbolism

- Ancient Predecessors: The Greek phalanx, with its tight formations and long spears, was a direct precursor to the later shield wall. Another powerful example is the Roman legions' iconic 'testudo' formation, with soldiers interlinking their shields overhead to create a protective 'shell' impervious to missiles. While the Middle Ages developed their own distinct variation, they did not invent the broad concept.

- Stamford Bridge (1066): This battle serves as a bridge between Viking shield wall tactics and their Anglo-Saxon inheritors. Here, the Saxons withstood a berserker charge from the legendary Harald Hardrada's Norse forces before succumbing to ill-considered pursuit that shattered their line and allowed the Vikings a hard-fought victory.

- The Battle of Hastings (1066): Perhaps the most legendary portrayal of the Anglo-Saxon shield wall. Harold Godwinson's forces held firm for hours against the varied assaults of William the Conqueror's Normans. It took tactical maneuvering and feigned retreats from the Normans to break that shield wall, allowing their cavalry to seize the victory.

Strengths of the Shield Wall: Strength in Unity

- The Battle of Maldon (991): Made immortalized in Anglo-Saxon poetry, this clash highlights the resilience of the shield wall. Facing a Viking raiding party, Ealdorman

THE ART OF MEDIEVAL WARFARE: STRATEGIES, TACTICS, AND WEAPONS OF THE BATTLEFIELD

Byrhtnoth's Saxon forces fought valiantly until eventually overwhelmed. Still, they inflicted casualties through a disciplined shield wall that the Vikings couldn't immediately break.

• Viking Raids: Much of the early Viking success owed to their use of the shield wall in conjunction with swift longships. These allowed sudden landings and a strong defensive core when raiding coastal settlements. The formation helped ensure their gains against often lightly armed villagers.

The Fall of the Shield Wall: Facing Changing Warfare

• Battle of Agincourt (1415): Here, the English longbow's devastating efficiency pierced holes in French ranks. Shield walls alone weren't sufficient against that rain of arrows. This, combined with narrow terrain and French overconfidence, led to a victory that underlined the waning dominance of purely melee-focused tactics.

• Hundred Years War: Battles like Crécy, Poitiers, and others highlight growing battlefield diversity. Instead of pitched confrontations decided by lines of infantry, cavalry charges, flanking, and ranged units grew in importance throughout this long conflict. It wasn't merely a single battle that destroyed the shield wall, but the war's evolution away from solely relying on heavily armored, tightly packed fighters.

• The Italian Wars (1494-1559): This series of conflicts marked a clear shift, as powerful pike formations of Swiss mercenaries and Spanish swordsmen became dominant.

They still favored close-order fighting, but the focus wasn't on solely defensive 'holding a line' as with the early shield wall. Instead, tactics emphasized movement and engaging the enemy – pushing further back against the older concept of static 'waiting battles'.

When Reach Ruled: The Long Rise of the Polearm

Polearms, broadly defined as hafted weapons with a long reach advantage, have their roots far back in military history. However, the truly defining period of their ascent and battlefield dominance falls squarely within the later Middle Ages and the early Renaissance. Several factors conspired to propel these weapons from occasionally used support tools to becoming the backbone of entire armies. Let's examine why and how polearms seized center stage.

Challenging the Mounted King

Throughout the early and high Middle Ages, the heavily armored knight epitomized battlefield might. These were individuals wielding superior equipment, trained from youth in warfare. The expense involved in outfitting these mounted warriors created a significant power imbalance between nobility and peasant foot soldiers.

The rise of polearms offered a counter to this dominance. Weapons like long pikes and halberds—the latter combining a spike, axe blade, and hook—granted far greater reach than a sword or battleaxe wielded from horseback. If a wall of these weapons could maintain formation, even the finest armor had a high chance of being unhorsed or mortally wounded before striking an effective blow. This potential tactical equalizer fueled much of the development of dedicated polearm tactics.

THE ART OF MEDIEVAL WARFARE: STRATEGIES, TACTICS, AND WEAPONS OF THE BATTLEFIELD

Discipline: The Critical Element

A single peasant with a spear, no matter how long, posed little threat to a trained knight. The true power of polearms emerged with the refinement of mass formations and strict discipline. The Swiss, in particular, gained legendary reputations for their use of long pikes in dense squares. Thousands of pointed spearheads bristling outwards at all angles proved incredibly effective in both deterring cavalry charges and grinding down armored infantry.

This success had less to do with individual courage and more with rigorous drills. To ensure a pike square moved smoothly as a unit and avoided creating fatal gaps within its ranks, incessant training was vital. It wasn't merely a peasant rebellion but an early example of professional fighting units built around a specific core weapon. The success of the Swiss model spread, making pike formations a sought-after element by kings and warlords across Europe.

Types of Polearms: Tool for Every Task

While the pike might be the most immediately recognizable example, it wasn't the only form of polearm that found military utility. Its variations and cousins added flexibility to any force relying on them:

- The Halberd: A multi-purpose weapon that provided piercing, slashing, and hooking options. Versatile against armored infantry and cavalry, halberds often flanked pike squares as their 'teeth' – breaking enemy formations engaged at the end of long pikes.

- Bills and Glaives: More humble in origin, these often adapted agricultural tools served an anti-cavalry role similar to pikes but generally focused on hooking and pulling horsemen from saddles. Their shorter length typically meant sacrificing outright stopping power against heavier plate armor.

- Poleaxes: These evolved towards greater sophistication as knightly combat shifted to being frequently on foot. Their combination of armor-piercing spike and hefty axe-like blades found them favor with those warriors still focused on direct, individual battles rather than large formations.

Formations & Tactics: More Than Pointy Sticks

Pike squares represent the most famous polearm tactic, but not the only one:

- Hedgehog Squares: These all-pike formations were incredibly strong defensively, able to face threats from every direction by rotating. This made them superb for open terrain as a last stand, or covering a slow retreat against encircling foes.

- Mixed Units: Pike squares became potent building blocks within complex army compositions. Protected flanks of crossbowmen or arquebusiers (early gunpowder firearms) maximized casualties dealt on an approaching foe. These units could form interlocking defensive patterns, supporting heavy cavalry strikes while ensuring enemy infantry struggled to simply wipe out an army without dedicated formations of their own.

Projectile Warfare's Shifting Tides

THE ART OF MEDIEVAL WARFARE: STRATEGIES, TACTICS, AND WEAPONS OF THE BATTLEFIELD

Beyond the obvious limits imposed by weather, a number of tactical and logistical drawbacks constrained archers and crossbowmen from completely dominating the battlefield.

- Ammunition Constraints: Whether crafted arrows or metal crossbow bolts, these were finite resources. An archer's quiver carried only so many shots, and while more could be carried during large battles, resupply mid-combat was difficult, if not impossible. Crossbowmen fared marginally better as bolts were easier to scavenge, but larger-scale siege scenarios could deplete the supply of quarrels too. In contrast, melee fighting remained effective as long as a soldier could still grip their weapon and had the strength to swing it.

- Indirect Engagement: Projectiles relied on an unobstructed arc towards their target. Defenses as simple as tall shields, formations holding tight overhead protection, or maneuvering behind natural terrain features rendered arrows significantly less effective. Siege situations often demanded clever deployment of archers to find 'openings' to angle in their shots, adding complexity, and reducing opportunities to achieve decisive damage through missiles alone.

- Morale's Edge: While an arrow through the eye was undeniably lethal, even well-armored foes might survive wounds from projectiles. Often, their impact focused more on inflicting casualties without ensuring absolute kills. In contrast, the visceral brutality of close combat–severed limbs, shattered bones– added a level of terror few volleys could achieve consistently. It's a key reason melee units continued to play such a vital role in breaking an enemy's will to fight after those initial barrages had passed.

- Skirmishers to Linebreakers: As battles escalated beyond early confrontations, projectiles transitioned from potentially battle-winning force to supporting element. Archers remained deadly at picking off fleeing, exposed flanks or softening opposing forces before full melee engagement. Crossbowmen, with their armor-piercing capability, held value in sieges and against elite, tightly packed infantry formations. However, neither could consistently 'win' a battle through their actions alone.

The Rise of Combined Arms and Projectiles' Legacy

The key turning point lay in the evolution of armies as composite forces rather than singular units. As we've discussed, knights, infantry, and projectile users had distinct strengths and weaknesses that became increasingly apparent. Effective commanders sought to blend their uses rather than rely solely on one:

- Archers behind spear/pike walls.

- Cavalry to exploit breaks created by archery and heavy infantry clashes.

- Crossbowmen weakening densely packed, high-value targets before heavier units engaged

Projectile warfare did not disappear. Bows persisted in specialist roles, particularly in Eastern empires alongside horse archers using hit-and-run tactics. The crossbow became a potent tool of urban defense and naval combat. Even the arrival of gunpowder wouldn't

THE ART OF MEDIEVAL WARFARE: STRATEGIES, TACTICS, AND WEAPONS OF THE BATTLEFIELD

immediately negate them; early battles often featured a curious mixture of bows, crossbows, and the first clumsy firearms.

- The Battle of Falkirk (1298): Often portrayed as an English longbow victory against William Wallace's Scottish forces, this narrative simplifies matters. Yes, Edward I's archers devastated the Scottish spearmen, but it was his disciplined knights who exploited that disarray to turn the tide decisively. This wasn't simply one arm winning then retreating, but a tactical transition in real-time. This highlights the value of flexibility, with different units fulfilling complementary roles within the same battle.

- Swiss Ascendancy Those near-impenetrable pike blocks proved devastating against traditional heavy cavalry charges—but also incredibly rigid. Swiss victories weren't guaranteed, as battles like Bicocca (1522) demonstrated. They were vulnerable to outmaneuvering or bombardment with early field artillery. Mercenary pikemen became formidable and feared, yet never an undefeatable 'one size fits all' solution on their own. This encouraged commanders to acquire various tools - the Swiss being merely one highly potent option among the wider arsenal.

- The Spanish Tercio: An iconic and potent force, Tercios combined swordsmen, pikemen, and some of the earliest effective arquebusiers (heavy, early musket users). It's the perfect encapsulation of this military evolution. Volleys were used to disrupt opposing formations, then their disciplined pikemen blocks created defensive hardpoints, with swordsmen surging out to engage disorganized lines. While not invincible, these formations emphasized synergy rather than dominance through purely cavalry or ranged power.

• Naval Evolution: While land tactics are more often showcased, a parallel evolution occurred at sea. Ships like the carrack carried an increasingly varied force of melee fighting crew, crossbowmen, and small cannons. Boarding actions remained core to their doctrine, yet this mix of forces allowed softening targets before that bloody climax. It showed flexibility was king, even within the often restrictive, close-quarters confines of a wooden ship.

Why Combined Arms Rose Over Specialist Forces

• Battlefield unpredictability: No commander could truly foresee exactly how each engagement would unfold. A force overly reliant on heavy cavalry would find itself stymied by cunning terrain use as at Bannockburn (1314). Alternatively, an all-archer army risked annihilation if closed upon swiftly, demonstrating reliance on a singular tactic is inherently brittle.

• Counterplay: As polearms rose, tactics to break squares were refined. Early firearms found ways to out-range longbows. For every advancement within a specialized fighting arm, a counter often soon followed. Combined arms aimed at mitigating those counters without entirely negating any component's advantage.

• Logistics and Cost: Not every lord could field massive forces of the knightly elite. But cheaper levied spearmen and training competent archers was attainable to more kingdoms. This practical element contributed as much as

THE ART OF MEDIEVAL WARFARE: STRATEGIES, TACTICS, AND WEAPONS OF THE BATTLEFIELD

purely tactical concerns - a diverse army simply allowed for a larger force without breaking the treasury.

Chapter 6: Siege Warfare: Breaking the Walls

Beyond Walls: Strategies and Goals of the Besieger

It's vital to remember that no besieged castle or city existed in absolute isolation. Therefore, besieging armies considered more than simply the physical strength of the defenses. Time was always the enemy of those trying to penetrate a fortress:

- Logistics and Supplies: Long sieges stretched supply lines beyond their limits. Armies foraging in hostile territory were vulnerable to raids and the simple reality of limited available food in any region. This encouraged attackers to utilize potentially riskier yet quicker methods, hoping for less of a prolonged war of attrition and greater chances of swift victory.

- Morale and Public Sentiment: For the besieger, drawn-out sieges chipped away at morale in their own ranks as resources and casualties increased. Defenders facing certain victory might offer terms before such desperation weakened the attackers' bargaining position. Conversely, news of nearby reinforcements or allies maneuvering to break the siege might force even well-armed attackers to make a risky gamble—launching a full assault while they held numerical superiority, however fleeting.

- Cost and Profit: Warfare costs money, a truth for both attackers and defenders. Besieging lords might accept lower ransom terms on a weakened yet largely whole town versus one reduced to burned-out rubble even after victory. Thus, there was a delicate balance between destruction and preservation - sufficient force to cow the defenders, yet not so devastating as to make the prize worthless upon success.

This complex dance of psychological factors, economic constraints, and military pragmatism heavily influenced which approaches proved most effective or were simply attempts out of desperation. Siege warfare was inherently more unpredictable than pitched battles.

Methodical Methods: Sapping, Mining, and Underhanded War

The slow attrition of sapping operations and the potential for sudden chaos unleashed by collapsing tunnels made this form of undermining an attractive option, regardless of whether it proved decisive. While requiring specialized forces with dangerous skill sets, its effects went beyond merely attempting to breach a section of wall.

Imagine being within a besieged city. It's easy to defend when every threat is visible atop the fortifications. With sappers at work, suspicion reigned supreme. Hearing those taps and echoes underground without knowing where or when an attack might materialize could quickly lead to frayed nerves and paranoia. Even a failed attempt could lead to defenders abandoning a previously uncompromised piece of their position out of fear, gifting the besiegers vital ground. It was warfare against sleep-deprived minds as much as the stone defenses themselves.

Ladders, Assault Towers and Bravado

While iconic, scaling tactics played a more nuanced role than purely storming forward in brute force assaults. These methods thrived in tandem with other elements of a siege operation:

- Diversion and Exhaustion: A large-scale scaling attempt drew defenders onto the battlements. If coupled with other ongoing methods like sapping or bombardment with missiles, a defender couldn't be everywhere at once. Smaller assault waves might find a weak point or breach left vulnerable, not through overwhelming power, but by ensuring every inch of the walls had to be guarded equally.

- Assault Towers: Pre-fabricated, these siege engines offered greater protection as ladders were built into a mobile protected framework. It could allow attackers to scale onto towers directly instead of the exposed sides of the curtain walls. Even then, these remained incredibly costly operations with defenders usually holding a distinct advantage against the bottlenecked flow of men emerging atop the siege tower.

Machines and the Rise of 'Specialist' Siege Warfare

Operating a massive battering ram or trebuchet required more than raw muscle. This led to siege engine crews becoming vital, in-demand soldiers – as essential for taking cities as swordsmen were for winning field battles.

Rams required coordinated teamwork, rhythm, and an almost battering stubbornness as fatigue set in. Trebuchet operation went beyond simply placing a rock and sending it soaring. Careful calculation of counterweights, sling length, and the type of ammunition hurled determined where, and with what effect, payloads flew. It transformed what initially appeared as merely crude hurling machinery into devices of semi-precise destruction when well-crewed.

Why Study Siege Methods?

While cities rarely fought alone, these tactics remain vital components of medieval warfare study:

THE ART OF MEDIEVAL WARFARE: STRATEGIES, TACTICS, AND WEAPONS OF THE BATTLEFIELD

- Rise of centralized control within kingdoms as monarchs recognized that defeating these walled bastions was pivotal to victory.

- The evolution of warfare beyond merely battles won with the charge or volley. Sieges showcase war as a contest of logistics, technology, and will.

- They highlight the brutal truths of life within these times - a reminder that, with walls up, it became the 'city', not an individual ruler who faced total loss when siege engines rolled forward.

Absolutely! Let's delve into the defensive side of siege warfare, examining ingenious countermeasures devised against seemingly overwhelming attackers. Keep in mind fortifications were never meant to be fully passive—defenders utilized tactics ranging from clever engineering to outright brutality to repel attacks. While walls held immense symbolic and material value, success or failure hinged on more than merely the height of stone or width of a moat.

Fortifications: Beyond Mere Stone & Wood

Medieval fortress design embraced an active, multi-layered defensive strategy. It's essential to consider them less as impenetrable barriers and more like deadly obstacle courses meant to inflict maximum casualties in specific kill zones. Let's examine some crucial elements involved:

- Concentricity: Rings of defense became increasingly common after exposure to Crusader castle designs. Inner and outer gates, multiple courtyards – defenders could fall back while still actively inflicting losses against attackers forced into tighter, exposed funnels.

- Murder Holes & Machicolations: Purpose-built openings along overhangs and above gates allowed defenders to pour missiles or burning liquid down onto attackers trying to batter through gates or packed below against a section of wall. They targeted those areas 'blind' to archers on the ramparts – ensuring no assault zone lay without potential counterattack.

- Moats & Ditches: More than slowing enemy advance, these served multiple purposes. Water-filled moats undermined attempts at sapping with tunnels, while dry ditches became potential killing zones when attackers descended only to find it impossible to swiftly scale those walls under direct fire.

- Tower Placement: Round replaced earlier square towers by the late Middle Ages. This reduced structural weak points and, crucially, eliminated blind spots defenders had to account for with square designs. Careful tower placement meant overlapping fields of fire for archers on those raised positions. Attackers found no 'safe' approach even during siege engine preparations.

It's vital to remember these designs evolved alongside siege methods themselves. As a trebuchet's range increased, walls became taller in response. Each development pushed a form of warfare technology arms race that ensured fortifications never grew truly obsolete within this era.

Defenders Strike Back: Going On the Offensive

THE ART OF MEDIEVAL WARFARE: STRATEGIES, TACTICS, AND WEAPONS OF THE BATTLEFIELD

Successful defense never meant staying wholly reactive and huddled behind stone. The best-led troops sought avenues to strike back through various methods, each carrying risks that could result in even a well-supplied fortress crumbling rapidly.

- Sallies: Not merely desperate last stands, sally attacks involved troops launching themselves directly out from the castle or city walls into the besiegers' camp or attack formations. The hope was to disrupt preparations, destroy critical siege engines like trebuchets, or demoralize enemies through inflicting a sharp, localized defeat. It usually demanded timing and surprise, often relying on small gates hidden in less obvious sectors of the fortifications. However, a poorly implemented sally could leave a position dangerously undermanned if repulsed.

- Fire as Weapon: Whether flaming arrows flung against vulnerable siege towers or pots of flammable liquid aimed at battering rams, fire attacks could quickly throw back a seemingly successful assault. These weren't merely about damaging wooden equipment but targeting vulnerable crew. A trebuchet might endure some flames, but its operators had little protection. Skilled and desperate defenders focused on targeting those irreplaceable skilled soldiers as siege methods advanced.

- Counter-Engineering: As highlighted previously, sappers digging below ground met defenders digging their own counter-tunnels. Underground skirmishes often devolved into brutal affairs for a few feet of earthen gain. Some of the earliest uses of primitive explosives within defensive tunnels emerged due to these desperate and claustrophobic struggles for control.

Mind vs. Might: Deception & Resilience

Siege warfare tested a defender's resolve through attrition, hunger, and disease. However, psychological tactics could bolster defense, or pave the way for the attacker's success.

- Displays of Plenty: Defenders dumping what appeared to be supplies over the walls served as a show of resistance. While potentially wasteful if a bluff, it aimed at breaking besieger morale by projecting an image of endurance against perceived odds. Conversely, some commanders sought to sow mistrust within the attacker's ranks, hinting at treachery within the defenders or claiming reinforcements were imminent – anything to make the besieging army question the practicality of continuing at great cost.

- Cruelty as Deterrent: Public torture and brutal public executions of captured attackers aimed to sow dread among enemy troops. While sometimes inspiring bloody reprisal actions if the fortress eventually fell, this act focused on creating fear as a defensive weapon by showing the high cost of potential failure for any individual soldier forced to attack those formidable walls.

- Fortification Examples

- Krak des Chevaliers (Syria): A quintessential illustration of Crusader castle engineering, this fortress held immense strategic value as the Knights Hospitaller defied Saladin's assaults in 1188. Its nested walls, rounded towers, and 'death zones' of overlapping fire perfectly showcase those principles of fortified design turning it into a costly proposition for attackers even on open terrain.

THE ART OF MEDIEVAL WARFARE: STRATEGIES, TACTICS, AND WEAPONS OF THE BATTLEFIELD

- Château de Coucy (France): Built during the 13th century, this castle boasted incredible walls – many exceeding 7 meters thick at their base. Even when sapping undermined part of a tower in 1537 during the Italian Wars, its massive construction limited the collapse. Moreover, its prominent placement and extensive artillery fortifications meant this siege could only truly succeed through betrayal from within, not direct conquest.

- Harlech Castle (Wales): Built under ambitious Edward I as part of his subjugation campaigns, this masterpiece of concentric defense played a role in successive Welsh rebellions. During the Wars of the Roses (15th century), its defenses withstood a lengthy siege, showcasing how layered design continued to frustrate potential conquerers even as siege methods evolved further.

Active Defense & Countermeasures

- Constantinople (Multiple Sieges): The famed capital of the Byzantine Empire fell only when cannons made walls truly obsolete. Its history includes valiant stands against Arab forces in the 7th and 8th centuries, highlighting sallies, defensive use of 'Greek Fire' (an early flamethrower), and chain defenses across straits used to destroy and trap attack fleets trying to storm from the sea. Its successive falls and survivals are intrinsically tied to both the city's formidable design and a willingness to actively push back, not just endure.

- Siege of Orléans (1428–29): This turning point in the Hundred Years' War saw iconic Joan of Arc rally defenders during a seemingly hopeless struggle. French sallies inflicted defeats outside the walls and disrupted attempts to create earthen siege mounds to overtop fortifications. Even after initial breaches were forced, her presence ensured morale held despite constant fighting, paving the way for a desperate relief army – and eventual lifting of the English siege entirely.

Psychological Impacts

- The Pale of Dublin: Medieval England held this tenuous, fortified enclave in Ireland under constant threat. During sieges of towns within the Pale, Irish troops were noted for mutilating captured soldiers' bodies, aiming to strike fear into reinforcements with tales of barbarity. While it didn't prevent losses, it contributed to English garrisons feeling isolated and increasingly reluctant to hold against overwhelming numbers.

- Vlad the Impaler (15th Century): His infamous tactic of impaling victims had strategic aims beyond torture. When the Ottoman Sultan Mehmed II found a forest of thousands of his soldiers so executed during his Wallachian campaign, while this did not deter his advance, it paints a stark picture of how calculated cruelty could inflict real dread in a besieging army.

It's vital to remember these sources may be biased to their particular victor. But even through those lenses, we see undeniable patterns and themes - siege warfare demanded incredible fortitude, resilience, and sometimes a willingness to match an attacker's brutality to prevent total defeat.

Part III: Weaponry and Technology

Chapter 7: Blades and Polearms: Close Combat

Blades of War: An Overview of Medieval Swords

The sword enjoys iconic status for a reason – its use extended far beyond warfare and into the realms of symbolism and personal status. However, in battle, a sword was a remarkably adaptable tool, with various designs tailored to specific purposes:

- Arming Swords: The classic one-handed blade. It provided a blend of speed, cutting power, and thrusting potential. Its versatility served knights on foot and horseback, though heavier designs emphasized slashing cuts. These remained in use from the early Middle Ages through to the later Renaissance.

- Longswords: Evolving as armor increased, longswords embraced greater length and two-handed grips. This provided leverage for both powerful cutting strokes, but also 'half-swording' techniques aimed at thrusting into gaps in plate armor. They became symbols of knightly status but weren't ubiquitous among all combatants due to their cost and the greater skill they demanded.

- Cavalry Swords: While lighter arming swords often played a backup role for mounted knights, specialized designs evolved. Some focused on a stronger stabbing point and were heavily weighted for powerful downward thrusts delivered from horseback. Later periods saw curved sabers gain use, emphasizing draw cuts while the rider charged past – reflecting battlefield role variations even within weapon classification.

- Greatswords: These massive two-handed weapons occupy a specific and fascinating niche. Too cumbersome for general melee, they found roles in the later medieval period – breaking up pike formations, guarding key positions, and sometimes as 'prestige' blades showcasing elite status more than everyday combat. It's crucial to remember they represent one particular extreme, not the universal battlefield sword.

Swords: Limitations & Battlefield Considerations

No weapon is flawless, and swords were no exception. Understanding their limits offers clarity into why battlefield roles shifted over the centuries:

- Armor: Even early mail made slashing wounds far less deadly. As armor advanced towards greater plate coverage, swords evolved to favor thrusting techniques aimed at tiny gaps. Yet a poorly placed attack against full plate would have negligible effect, encouraging mixed-force tactics using other weapons in tandem.

- Reach: Sword combat necessitates dangerous proximity. Its reliance on single, committed, precise blows put the wielder at constant risk against longer reach alternatives like spears or later pikes. This limitation drove the development of formations maximizing a group of swordsmen's effectiveness compared to the raw reach advantage of their foes.

- Cost & Training: Compared to a spear or simple axe, a well-made sword was incredibly expensive. Training to use it skillfully took even longer. This restricted sword use in large-scale armies, though they persisted among individual knights or later mercenary groups with the funds to outfit themselves appropriately.

Axes: Brutal Efficiency on the Battlefield

Often falsely depicted as crude barbarian tools, battle axes had distinct benefits on a budget-conscious battlefield:

- Armor Piercing: Many axes sported a focused spike opposite the broad cutting edge. This concentrated force onto a tiny surface area, making it more effective than a glancing sword blow against chainmail or even some plate elements. They were less costly to produce than a complex sword hilt and blade.

- Hooking Function: Certain designs evolved to catch a foe's shield or weapon as part of a disarm attempt. These could also assist in pulling riders from their saddles – proving that an axe had battlefield functions far beyond merely hacking at the enemy.

- Simplicity & Power: While advanced techniques existed, wielding an axe required less finesse than mastering swordplay. A heavy axeblow with full arm strength carried the potential to incapacitate a foe regardless of precisely where it landed. This made them suitable for levies of peasant foot soldiers in addition to more skilled warriors.

Maces: When Blunt Force Wins Battles

The mace capitalized on another approach in dealing with battlefield armor:

- Plate Buster: A weighty mace delivered with full force could dent or cave in plates even when it couldn't penetrate with a cutting or piercing action. The shock of the impact alone could stun and disorient foes – opening openings for further decisive attacks.

- Helmet Focused: Unlike a broadsword swing, a mace concentrated all its force into a tiny hitting surface. This made them very effective in targeting helmets, even those well-constructed. The force could inflict concussions or cause debilitating neck injuries indirectly by violently snapping the wearer's head back.

- Varied Forms: From simple flanged designs to elaborate spiked variants, maces allowed for both blunt force impacts and potentially impaling secondary functions. They found niches among cavalry to batter against foe's helmets at close range, while infantry versions became favored in battles where large bodies of tightly packed enemies offered vulnerable, slower-moving targets.

The Rise of the Long Weapon: Reach as a Battle Changer

The appeal of polearms – spears, halberds, glaives, and many more – boils down to one core concept: keeping yourself alive by keeping your attacker further away. The evolution of weapons is, in many ways, an evolution of reach. This has numerous battlefield implications:

THE ART OF MEDIEVAL WARFARE: STRATEGIES, TACTICS, AND WEAPONS OF THE BATTLEFIELD

- Countering Cavalry: While not impenetrable, a bristling line of spearheads presented a serious deterrent to any horsemen contemplating a reckless charge. Even armored knights and horses lacked the mass to push through such formations unscathed. Polearms gave foot soldiers a vital tool against a seemingly superior form of warfare, upending long-established battlefield hierarchies.

- Anti-Infantry Effectiveness: Reach is just as valuable against foes on foot. A swordsman must close a considerable distance to become effective, all the while facing the ever-present danger of impalement on a polearm held at the ready. Halberds, with their various spikes and blades, presented multiple offensive threats simultaneously, further increasing the complexity of approaching someone so equipped.

- Ease of Use (Comparatively): While expert formations required immense drilling, training a foot soldier in basic spear tactics took dramatically less time than crafting a skilled swordsman. Polearms helped level the playing field when large, hastily recruited forces took to the battlefield. A peasant with basic instruction could threaten elite armored infantry due to that added measure of distance.

But It's About More Than Length...

The effectiveness of polearms cannot be reduced to merely having a pointy stick on a longer handle. It was advancements in tactics and their utilization within larger battles that truly revolutionized medieval combat:

- Pike Squares: Densely packed troops wielding exceptionally long pikes became synonymous with Swiss mercenaries and later copied by numerous forces. Moving as a disciplined block, rotating ranks to bring fresh troops into the front, these squares were nightmares to infantry or cavalry unprepared to face them. It showcased how polearms maximized effectiveness not through singular heroes but through formation fighting.

• Combined Arms Synergy Pike blocks weren't invincible. Enter halberdiers: Their weapon combo was the 'teeth' of many military forces. If enemies engaged the dense pikes, these units countered, breaking open gaps or flanking. Other tools like billhooks were equally vital to drag riders from saddles, further exploiting openings to ensure cavalry did not simply go around vulnerable pike formations.

• Evolving Battlefield Role: Early battles show even basic spear or axe-wielding groups could use reach to disrupt charges or hold foes long enough for heavier hitters to engage. As polearms grew more specialized (longer shafts, additional weapon elements), battles featured 'lines' of soldiers where some troops focused on holding ground, others on exploiting any break in ranks caused by those simpler yet essential spearmen.

Limits & Why Swords Persisted

Polearms didn't magically turn warfare into a game won solely by who possessed the longest reach. Limitations abound:

• Formation Dependency: A single pikeman caught alone was in just as much trouble as the loneliest swordsman. Polearm power flowed from their use in disciplined units drilled to work seamlessly together. In close quarters where those formations broke down, their dominance faltered rapidly.

- Terrain Matters: Tight corridors, like dense forests or within towns, nullified reach. Even gentle hills upset the rhythm of a pike thrust, opening vulnerabilities when that perfect bristling square lost cohesion. Swordsmen persisted for these situations where maneuverability mattered more than the safety of added distance between combatants.

- Armor Still an Important Factor: Polearms became superb equalizers. Yet, a truly well-made full plate still afforded significant protection and could withstand direct pike thrusts. Swords gained specialized half-swording grip techniques explicitly intended to find those tiny 'chinks' in armored protection with precision strikes even during melee.

The Polearm Legacy

As gunpowder weaponry rose in prominence, the age of polearms slowly, inevitably faded. Yet, their impact lingered; even during the era of muskets, bayonets attached to firearms acted as desperate last-resort spears—a brutal homage to their predecessors. They also solidified several truths about battlefield evolution:

- Sometimes, simple solutions are remarkably potent.

- It's how troops are used, not just what they're armed with, that matters

- Warfare is an 'arms race' with no truly final victor—every advance eventually breeds a countermeasure.

Absolutely! Here's a deep dive into the intricate connections between armor and weapons development, specifically tailored for the context of your medieval war tactics book. I'll focus on the core period of medieval warfare for this piece.

The Medieval Period: Armor as a Catalyst for Battlefield Evolution

Medieval Europe witnessed a remarkable dance between technological innovation and tactical shifts spurred by the ever-evolving nature of battlefield protection. From the early chainmail-clad warrior to the late period's shining knight encased in full plate armor, defensive capabilities drove profound changes in the design and deployment of weapons across the ages.

Chainmail: Flexibility vs. Piercing Power

Early medieval combat was defined by the widespread use of chainmail. Relatively lightweight and flexible, chainmail offered decent protection against the cuts and slashes of swords and axes – the dominant weapons of the era. While relatively resistant to slicing, chainmail's interwoven rings could be penetrated by strong thrusts and piercing weapons.

This weakness triggered a pivotal response within battlefield arsenals. Weapon design honed in on penetrating, pointed designs such as spears and specialized "bodkin" arrowheads with their armor-piercing capability. The rise of powerful longbows and crossbows during this period further illustrates this tactical arms race - volleys of these lethal projectiles could defeat most chainmail at significant distances. The dominance of mail also incentivized the design of heavy-hitting blunt force weapons such as the flail and mace, aiming to inflict shock damage through the armor rather than penetrate it directly.

The Emergence of Plate: Thrusting, Crushing, and Piercing

THE ART OF MEDIEVAL WARFARE: STRATEGIES, TACTICS, AND WEAPONS OF THE BATTLEFIELD

The 14th and 15th centuries introduced the game-changer: plate armor. This full-body protection rendered traditional cut-and-thrust attacks significantly less effective. As chainmail was gradually phased out, smiths were challenged to find weapons that could reliably overcome the resilience of steel plates.

Weapons shifted to prioritize devastating blunt force, exploiting plate armor's limitations in areas of coverage. Warhammers became prevalent, with their focus on delivering blows capable of crumpling steel, denting joints, and inflicting internal damage that armor could not entirely prevent. Polearms such as halberds and poleaxes grew in popularity, leveraging their length and multiple striking surfaces to bypass armor with blows to vulnerable areas – particularly neck, armpits, and legs.

However, as metalworking refined the shape and composition of plate armor, sword designs adapted. Blades evolved to take on stiffer forms, optimizing the profile for powerful thrusts. Weapons like the rapier emerged, emphasizing agility and the ability to find those precious unprotected gaps in an opponent's plates.

Beyond the Sword: Armor's Indirect Influence

The influence of armor development didn't solely impact the shape and capabilities of individual weapons. It also indirectly affected broader military tactics and the role of different forces on the battlefield:

- Infantry Revival: As armor offered increased protection, the prominence of foot soldiers saw a resurgence in medieval warfare. Armored knights dismounted on the battlefield, utilizing their formidable protection in close-quarters combat. Tactics adapted to focus on exploiting openings in enemy formations to pierce armored foes with specialized tools.

- **Cavalry Adaptation:** Though the mounted charge remained vital to tactical doctrine, heavier armor rendered horses more vulnerable to piercing weapons. Tactics adjusted to incorporate mounted archers and lancers, aiming to weaken and disrupt enemy formations rather than rely solely on the shock of a heavy charge.

- **Siege Warfare Evolution:** Advances in armor weren't just limited to individual warriors. Castles and fortifications received significant improvement due to the changing nature of offensive weapons. Engineers employed thicker walls, rounded bastions, and creative designs to mitigate the impact of ever-improving siege engines.

The Advent of Gunpowder: The Demise of the Armored Knight

While the impact of firearms was gradual, the introduction of gunpowder marked a shift away from heavy plate armor on the battlefield. While early firearms lacked range and accuracy, their armor-piercing potential outmatched the defenses available at the time. As technology advanced, firearms became less cumbersome and increasingly lethal, effectively turning the knight in shining armor into an endangered species. Eventually, plate armor became impractical against the relentless power of muskets and cannons.

The fascinating link between armor and weapons in the medieval world underscores the interconnectedness of warfare technology. These weren't isolated developments but interconnected facets of an ongoing competition on the battlefield. As protection improved, so too did the need to breach it, resulting in an impressive cascade of innovations, adaptations, and ultimately, profound changes in battlefield dynamics.

Let's dive into some specific historical examples that illustrate the use of these weapons on the medieval battlefield:

THE ART OF MEDIEVAL WARFARE: STRATEGIES, TACTICS, AND WEAPONS OF THE BATTLEFIELD

Swords

- Arming Sword & The Battle of Hastings (1066): The Norman Conquest saw widespread use of arming swords by both Saxon and Norman infantry. These blades were used for hacking at chainmail and leather armor, as well as for deadly thrusts when opportunities arose.

- Longsword & the Hundred Years' War (1337 - 1453): Battles like Agincourt and Crécy highlight the longsword's versatility. Knights dismounted, using it for vicious stabbing attacks into gaps in French plate armor or wielding it two-handed against less heavily armored opponents.

- Falchion & the Crusades (1095-1291): While less common than other swords, the falchion found favor with some knights for its powerful strikes. Some accounts cite these weapons effectively cleaving through lighter Saracen armor during the Crusades.

Axes

- Dane Axe & the Viking Age (8th-11th centuries): Saxon raiders striking against England wielded their iconic Dane axes to devastating effect. While chainmail offered some defense, the sheer power of these two-handed weapons left many a shield splintered and warriors felled.

- Battle Axe & the Battle of Bannockburn (1314): Robert the Bruce's Scottish troops expertly wielded battle axes alongside spears in a formation known as the schiltron. These short-hafted axes found purchase in the gaps of English armor, allowing the Scots to win a shocking victory.

Maces & Hammers

- Mace & The Mongol Invasions (13th century): Both European and Mongol horsemen utilized maces in the chaos of cavalry combat. Maces were particularly effective in inflicting concussive blows through helmets and lighter armor common in Eastern Europe.

- Warhammer & the Italian Wars (1494-1559): Battles like Fornovo saw the warhammer carried by armored knights and cavalry. As full plate armor became increasingly refined, the warhammer's armor-piercing spike was one of the few weapons with a chance of delivering a lethal blow.

Polearms

- Halberd & the Swiss Pikemen (14th-16th centuries): Battles like Sempach and Morgarten showed the Swiss using halberds alongside their iconic pikes. This deadly weapon could snag fully armored knights, pulling them from their horses to expose them to vulnerable thrusts and strikes.

- Billhook & the Peasants' Revolt (1381): While a simple tool, the billhook in the hands of rebelling English peasants proved an effective makeshift polearm, allowing them to unhorse armored knights and deal vicious blows against weaker points in armor.

Chapter 8: The Bow, Crossbow, and Beyond

The English Longbow: More Than Just a Weapon

In the hands of well-trained archers, the English longbow wasn't merely a powerful weapon; it was a catalyst for a radical shift in the dynamics of medieval battle. Its exceptional range, penetrating power, and the ease with which massed volleys could be unleashed redefined the relationship between infantry and the battlefield elite – the heavily armored knight.

The Weapon Itself: Simple Design, Devastating Effect

While crafted from humble yew wood, the English longbow possessed remarkable power. Standing approximately six feet tall, it was designed for a high draw weight, often exceeding 100 pounds of force. Traditional broadhead arrows were replaced with specialized "bodkin" points, possessing needle-like tips that maximized penetration even against steel breastplates.

Skilled longbowmen were products of a unique combination of cultural values and rigorous training. English law mandated regular archery practice for males of fighting age. It was this cultural devotion to the bow that gave England a strategic advantage, creating a ready pool of archers capable of launching up to a dozen arrows per minute, significantly more than the rate of their crossbow-wielding counterparts.

A New Paradigm on the Battlefield

Prior to the widespread adoption of the longbow, battles were often brutal slogs dominated by melee combat. Heavy cavalry charges carried immense force, often aimed at breaking enemy infantry formations through sheer shock and the momentum of armored horse and rider. The English longbow altered this dynamic, empowering common foot soldiers against this aristocratic dominance.

Battles like Crécy (1346) and Agincourt (1415) during the Hundred Years' War stand as testaments to the longbow's tactical potency. Here are the major ways the longbow changed warfare:

1. Area Denial: A storm of arrows, loosed at high arcs, turned approach routes into killing zones. Dense volleys inflicted casualties against even well-armored knights, disrupting charges and shattering the psychological certainty of a cavalry assault.
2. Anti-Armor Focus: Bodkin point arrows were exceptionally effective in piercing the relatively weaker chainmail or early plate armor commonly worn by French knights. Even when heavier plate armor became standard, arrows could still target unarmored horses, throwing heavy cavalry into disarray.
3. Defensive Superiority: English tactics often exploited terrain and fortifications to protect archers from direct engagement. Sharpened stakes angled outwards further negated cavalry charges, leaving knights and soldiers alike vulnerable to arrow fire while struggling to close the distance.
4. Shifting Importance of Infantry: The longbow was essentially an 'equalizer'. Lightly armored archers had newfound value as they could bring down formidable armor-clad foes. Instead of mere fodder for the clash of swords, foot soldiers became crucial to securing victory – a massive realignment of battlefield hierarchy.

Limits and Adaptations

Like any weapon, the longbow possessed limitations. It was reliant on the skill of its users, with years required to develop strength and accuracy. Maintaining supplies of quality arrows remained a logistical challenge. Furthermore, as the French became acutely aware of this threat, their reactions revealed evolving counter-tactics:

- Improved Armor: Advances in plate armor design rendered archers less reliably lethal. Arrows would still find exposed joints and areas with lighter plating, but the advantage began to erode.

- Cavalry Tactics: Instead of full-frontal charges, cavalry adapted to more harassing tactics with smaller groups. This increased maneuverability while aiming to provoke disorganized responses from the archer lines.

- Combined Arms Warfare: French military doctrine integrated longbow tactics with a focus on dismounted men-at-arms, crossbowmen, and later, gunpowder weapons. Battles grew more complex, relying on interplay between various forces.

Legacy of the Longbow

While eventually outpaced by firearms, the English longbow's time on the battlefield left an enduring mark on history. It exposed a significant vulnerability of the armored knight – a cornerstone of medieval power structures. More importantly, it showcased tactical innovation and its power to disrupt traditional battlefield dominance.

Even after its practical use declined, the longbow maintained cultural significance in England, symbolizing martial prowess and the potential of seemingly 'common' warriors to overcome seemingly insurmountable odds. The victories it wrought during the Hundred

Years' War solidified its place in myth and legend, contributing to the English national identity as masters of a weapon that forever changed the art of war.

Absolutely! Let's explore the crossbow, a weapon whose introduction sparked tactical change and debate that echoes through the ages of medieval warfare:

The Crossbow: Weapon of Controversy, Weapon of Change

Unlike the yew longbow, whose fame is intrinsically tied to England, the crossbow stands as a pan-European phenomenon. Though precursors existed earlier, the true medieval crossbow emerged around the 10th century. As a weapon employing mechanical advantage, it carried both notable benefits and a unique set of tactical considerations.

The Basics of the Crossbow

At its core, a crossbow features a horizontal bow (the 'prod') mounted on a stock (the 'tiller'). Its mechanical design offered numerous advantages over traditional bows:

- Ease of Use: While mastering accurate long-distance shooting remained a skill, the crossbow didn't require the archer's draw strength. A soldier could be trained relatively quickly in its basic operation.

- Sustained Aim: Crossbows employed mechanical means (levers, winches, or simple hooks called 'nuts') to draw and secure the bowstring. The archer remained at full draw effortlessly, ensuring steadier aim before releasing a shot.

- Powerful Bolts: Crossbows fired shorter projectiles called 'bolts' or 'quarrels'. Their denser design, combined with the propulsive force, significantly increased armor-piercing potential compared to traditional arrows.

These distinct advantages led to two major streams of thought regarding the crossbow in medieval warfare: a tactical asset or a threat to chivalry itself?

Tactical Realities: Advantages and Considerations

From a purely pragmatic perspective, crossbows found applications in several battlefield scenarios:

- Siege Warfare: The crossbow's accuracy and power from fixed positions made it effective for both defenders on castle walls and as a siege weapon itself, particularly through use of larger siege crossbows.

- Mounted Troops: Their ease of handling made crossbows well-suited for mounted units, such as the mercenary crossbow cavalry employed by Italian city-states during the Late Middle Ages.

- Anti-armor Capability: While their rate of fire was slow compared to a longbow, crossbow bolts had greater potential to penetrate chainmail and early plate armor, rendering even knightly protection suspect.

However, several disadvantages tempered the crossbow's dominance of the battlefield:

- Slow Reload: Mechanical aids allowed for powerful draws, but these took time. Even skilled crossbowmen rarely sustained rates of fire beyond a few shots per minute – slow compared to an archer's volleys.

- Vulnerability in Melee: Once a crossbowman fired their bolt, they became a liability in close quarters. Specialization arose, where crossbowmen were partnered with men-at-arms wielding pikes or shields for protection.

- Logistics and Costs: Compared to a relatively simple longbow, crossbows were complex mechanisms to create and maintain. Crafting the strong but flexible prod as well as the reliable trigger systems proved both time-consuming and expensive.

Chivalry and the Crossbow Controversy

Beyond tactical arguments, the crossbow generated strong emotional responses. To some, it symbolized the degradation of the knightly ideal. A noble knight could be slain by a relatively low-born peasant – a profound upheaval of battlefield order. This sentiment led Pope Innocent II to unsuccessfully attempt to ban crossbow use between Christian armies in the 12th century.

While this attempted prohibition held little tangible consequence, it demonstrates the crossbow's role in disrupting preconceptions of 'honorable' warfare - a debate with echoes from historical periods long after the Middle Ages.

Crossbows through the Medieval Period

As with armor, innovations in crossbows spurred tactical adaptation throughout the medieval era:

- Early Crossbows: These possessed short range and moderate armor-piercing capability. Their main roles were as defensive weapons or light skirmishing forces against less-armored units.

- Arbalest: Emerging in the 12th century, these possessed greater power due to increased prod strength. While often requiring mechanical aids for loading, the arbalest could overcome better armor at significant distances. These also started seeing more widespread use in cavalry units.

- Composite Prods: Incorporating horn and sinew to increase power, composite products made crossbows even more formidable on the battlefield. Yet, the difficulty and cost of manufacturing these limited their mass adoption.

- Late Medieval Advancements: Mechanisms like the cranequin made it feasible for soldiers to reload on the battlefield without excessive assistance. Foot troops armed with crossbows and shields become vital to supporting heavier troops.

Enduring Legacy

Even as firearms rose to dominate warfare, the crossbow remained a specialized weapon – its silence and accuracy valued by hunters and elite forces. The concept of a mechanical force multiplier persisted, eventually resurfacing in modern military crossbows. The crossbow's influence transcended battles, sparking discussion around battlefield ethics and the relentless progression of weapon technology – themes as relevant today as they were in the smoke-filled fields of medieval battle.

Absolutely! Let's add some historical context to enrich our understanding of the crossbow in medieval warfare. Here are a few key areas to consider:

The Rise of the Crossbow in a Changing World

- Urbanization and Mercenaries: From the 11th century onward, Europe saw the growth of towns and trade. Powerful city-states, especially in Italy, raised professional armies composed largely of mercenaries. Crossbows proved an efficient weapon in their hands, particularly in sieges and for defensive duties on city walls.

- Crusades: Constant conflict in the Holy Land brought Western military powers into contact with Eastern weapons. The more powerful siege crossbows employed by the Byzantines likely spurred an interest in developing more potent varieties back in Europe.

Specific Battles and Their Influence

- Battle of Hastings (1066): While still considered early in crossbow development, accounts hint at their usage by some Norman forces. This battle highlights how warfare was still a chaotic arena where traditional shock tactics met early examples of new technology.

- Battle of Legnano (1176): This conflict pitted the Lombard League of Italian cities against Germanic Emperor Frederick Barbarossa. Historical accounts speak of massed crossbow formations inflicting significant damage upon the imperial knights.

- Hundred Years' War (1337-1453): Both English and especially French armies utilized crossbows heavily. Initially effective against armored opponents, it showcases the ongoing back-and-forth adaptation between armor and weapons across a series of conflicts.

Beyond the Battlefield: Social and Political Shifts

- **Threats to Existing Order:** The outcry regarding the crossbow wasn't simply sour grapes by the knightly class. Powerful, easily learned weapons in the hands of urban militias threatened established power structures. The ability of peasant levies to challenge knightly prowess on the battlefield was profoundly disruptive.

- **Innovation and Regulation:** Crossbows acted as a catalyst for regulations of war and a re-evaluation of 'ideal' battlefield conduct. Some treaties forbade the use of particular crossbow variations like heavy siege models, revealing attempts to balance technological gains against perceived notions of honor.

Broader Technological Considerations

- **Gunpowder's Arrival:** Early firearms (especially the arquebus) became competitors to the crossbow. They eventually offered superior armor penetration and were relatively easier for armies to field in large numbers, marking the crossbow's gradual decline as a common battlefield weapon.

- **Technological Progression:** The crossbow highlights a pattern: when faced with a novel weapon, military powers rarely abandon an earlier mode of warfare outright. Instead, we see attempts to counter threats, adjust tactics, and refine new combinations of forces, fueling an arms race with no ultimate endpoint.

Chivalry and the Crossbow Controversy

Beyond tactical arguments, the crossbow generated strong emotional responses. To some, it symbolized the degradation of the knightly ideal.

A noble knight could be slain by a relatively low-born peasant – a profound upheaval of battlefield order. This sentiment stemmed partially from incidents like the Battle of Legnano (1176), where armies of Italian cities inflicted damaging defeats on Emperor Frederick Barbarossa's forces primarily through the use of crossbows. Pope Innocent II's attempted (and ultimately unsuccessful) ban on crossbow use between Christian armies in the 12th century reflects this anxiety about the erosion of battlefield conventions.

Absolutely! Let's explore the smoky rise of gunpowder weapons and their transformative, yet surprisingly gradual, introduction to the battlefields of medieval Europe.

The Spark of a Revolution: Gunpowder on the Medieval Stage

While their impact reverberates deeply in how we imagine war, the arrival of gunpowder weapons on the medieval scene was less a meteoric explosion and more a slow, uncertain burn. Early guns weren't battlefield dominators in their initial forms but rather tools that demanded innovation, tactical changes, and often a healthy dose of luck to achieve a decisive advantage.

Humble Beginnings: Cannons, Bombards, and Handgonnes

The very first European firearms emerged in the 13th century. Far from what we'd recognize as a gun, these were essentially metal tubes or rudimentary cannons:

- Bombards: Large, bulky, and notoriously unpredictable, bombards primarily found use in siege warfare. Stone balls or primitive metal shot created more noise and debris than accurate targeting, offering psychological terror against a city's defenders as much as physical destruction.

- Handgonnes: The precursors to hand-held firearms, these were little more than metal tubes strapped to wood. Igniting powder through a touch hole, they fired lead shot and often the gunner just as much as the intended target.

These simple yet impactful inventions faced hurdles beyond basic technology:

- Quality of Gunpowder: Early gunpowder was unstable, highly susceptible to moisture, and could be of very inconsistent granulation. Misfires and unexpected explosions could be as dangerous to the fire as the target.

- Production and Cost: Crafting decent quality cannons or even primitive handguns was an expensive, difficult process. These weren't weapons wielded by common infantry in vast numbers, but limited to wealthy cities or under the patronage of monarchs seeking an edge.

- Battlefield Application: Early gunners essentially became specialized siege engineers or highly vulnerable skirmishers. The slow rates of fire, inaccuracy, and lack of battlefield maneuverability meant they remained supplemental, not a replacement for existing forces.

The Evolution of Fire on the Battlefield

While initially offering more potential than practical dominance, firearms continued to evolve over centuries of medieval conflict. Here's where tactics gradually evolved along with the technology:

- Artillery Dominance: Improvements in cannon design and the refinement of gunpowder meant castles and fortifications, once bastions of defensive strength, now faced potential demolition from afar. Tactics focused heavily on the development of counter-artillery tactics and new fortification designs emphasizing round bastions rather than square towers to deflect shots.

- Birth of the Musket: While still cumbersome and inaccurate, the matchlock musket emerged in the 15th century, heralding a significant evolution in handheld arms. Battles like Cerignola (1503) showcased the musket in use by Spanish forces, where a mix of firepower and field defenses gave them a surprise victory over heavily armored French knights.

- Infantry Transformation: Initially utilized by highly trained units within larger armies, the advent of firearms eventually democratized war in a manner unforeseen by crossbow-wielding nobility. Armies with masses of musketeers began to supplant knightly dominance, requiring shifts in infantry tactics to protect those vulnerable during long reloads.

Lingering Limitations and Hybrid Weaponry

It's important to emphasize that adoption wasn't instantaneous. Several inherent drawbacks kept firearms from fully displacing earlier battlefield options:

- Rate of Fire: Reloading remained agonizingly slow, especially under stress. Tactics like continuous volley fire emerged to mitigate this, where lines of musketeers could maintain relatively constant fire. However, even this left armies vulnerable to swift attacks like a cavalry charge.

THE ART OF MEDIEVAL WARFARE: STRATEGIES, TACTICS, AND WEAPONS OF THE BATTLEFIELD

- Unpredictability: Accidents remained common. Moisture could render powder and matchcords useless, negating an army's firepower advantage in bad weather.

- Close-Combat Weakness: Even as bayonets transformed muskets into makeshift spears, firearm-equipped units in melee relied on supporting forces, particularly pikemen, for essential protection.

Throughout this period, warfare often blended 'old' with 'new'. Swords and polearms didn't vanish overnight, even alongside the smoke and thunder of matchlocks and cannons. Tactics revolved around combined arms forces, showcasing an ongoing tension between traditional arms and emerging technology.

Beyond Battle: Gunpowder's Ripple Effect

Firearms had far-reaching ramifications outside siege lines and clashes of armies:

- Changing Power Dynamics: Monarchs increasingly favored large, permanent armies equipped with standardized firearms. This eroded the regional power of smaller lords and knights who relied on their own resources.

- Revolution in War Funding: Firearms, cannons, and gunpowder were exceedingly expensive. The sheer economic power needed to field armies became an extension of warfare as much as actual combat.

- Technological Progress: The pursuit of better-performing firearms drove developments in metallurgy, chemistry, and precision tooling. These advances bled into other spheres of science and innovation beyond pure warfare.

Conclusion

The battlefields of medieval Europe were not static arenas. They served as proving grounds where the relentless tide of innovation clashed with the pressing need for tactical adaptation. The evolution of weaponry was a driving force in this dynamic. Chainmail's flexibility, once sufficient for deflecting slashing attacks, gave way to the increasing dominance of thrusting blades designed to penetrate vital gaps in rigid plate armor. This escalation underscores how battlefield gains were fleeting – every breakthrough in offensive power triggered a defensive countermeasure. Polearms, in their myriad forms, emerged from the recognition that battlefield supremacy depended on both reach and power – whether grappling armored knights from horses with hooked halberds or shattering helmets with focused warhammer blows.

With the English longbow came a radical rebalance of battlefield influence. No longer was mounted heavy cavalry the unchallenged force. Skillfully wielded longbows allowed massed archery volleys to devastate armored columns even at exceptional distances. The longbow's success wasn't simply due to its power but in transforming lightly armored peasant levies into lethal battlefield threats. These weapons advancements forced adaptations to the very foundation of combat, where combined-arms tactics sought to exploit strengths and overcome weaknesses through carefully timed charges, defensive barriers, and a measured understanding of what each weapon type offered.

And within the thunderous arrival of early cannons and firearms, one witnesses the seeds of even greater warfare upheaval. No longer confined to melee range, battles could be decided from greater distances. Castles faced potential obliteration from powerful siege bombardment, leading to innovative fortification modifications – a

THE ART OF MEDIEVAL WARFARE: STRATEGIES, TACTICS, AND WEAPONS OF THE BATTLEFIELD

cycle of destruction and reinvention on an even greater scale. Throughout this era, medieval warfare illustrates that advancement was neither constant nor inevitable. Instead, it was a series of gambits and responses, shaped as much by necessity and ingenuity as by emerging technologies.

www.ingramcontent.com/pod-product-compliance
Ingram Content Group UK Ltd.
Pitfield, Milton Keynes, MK11 3LW, UK
UKHW020206270125
454178UK00010B/467